普通高中课程标准实验教科书

英语

⊙ 总主编　戴炜栋　吴友富

（全国外国语学校系列教材）

任意选修课系列

主编　虞建华

英语戏剧与表演入门

教师用书

Teacher's Book

梅　丽编

Appreciation and Performance of English Drama:
A Basic Course

上海外语教育出版社

图书在版编目(CIP)数据

英语戏剧与表演入门 / 梅丽编.
—上海:上海外语教育出版社,2006
英语(全国外国语学校系列教材)任意选修课系列
教师用书
ISBN 7-5446-0175-7

I. 英… II. 梅… III. 英语—戏剧—高中—教学
参考资料 IV. G633.413

中国版本图书馆 CIP 数据核字(2006)第 080431 号

出版发行:上海外语教育出版社
　　　　　(上海外国语大学内)　邮编:200083
电　　话:021-65425300(总机),35051812(发行部)
电子邮箱:bookinfo@sflep.com.cn
网　　址:http://www.sflep.com.cn　http://www.sflep.com
责任编辑:陶　怡

印　　刷:上海华业装璜印刷厂
经　　销:新华书店上海发行所
开　　本:787×1092　1/16　印张 5.75　字数 115 千字
版　　次:2006 年 9 月第 1 版　2006 年 9 月第 1 次印刷
印　　数:2 100 册

书　　号:ISBN 7-5446-0175-7 / G · 0097
定　　价:9.00 元
本版图书如有印装质量问题,可向本社调换

英　语

（全国外国语学校系列教材）

总主编　戴炜栋　吴友富

编委会名单　（以姓氏笔画为序）

丁安仁	洛阳外国语学校	孔义川	保定外国语学校
王文龙	上海外国语大学双语学校	王全栓	太原外国语学校
王秀英	南昌外国语学校	王法明	兰州外国语学校
王建伟	成都外国语学校	王家祥	宁波外国语学校
王继慧	长春外国语学校	王　镎	常熟外国语学校
王瑞新	唐山外国语学校	毛　杰	郑州外国语学校
刘新来	广西师范大学附属外国语学校	刘淑云	济南外国语学校
刘世平	广东外语外贸大学附设外国语学校	朱建国	上海外国语大学附属浦东外国语学校
许永华	张家港外国语学校	杨云峰	云南大学附属外国语学校
杨能生	成都三原外国语学校	肖明华	成都实验外国语学校
张　玲	太原第二外国语学校	张裕云	重庆外国语学校
张奎文	天津外国语学校	林卫民	杭州外国语学校
郑　郁	临海外国语学校	周建民	乌鲁木齐外国语学校
赵建庭	西安外国语学校	赵继容	厦门外国语学校
段火香	九江外国语学校	郝又明	北京朝阳外国语学校
崔德明	上海外国语大学附属外国语学校	尉小珑	北京西城外国语学校
		曹伦华	苏州外国语学校
龚国祥	深圳外国语学校	强新志	石家庄外国语学校
董正璟	南京外国语学校	燕玲春	长沙外国语学校
燕华兴	武汉外国语学校		

前　言

　　21世纪是知识经济的时代。知识经济的主要特征就是经济和信息的全球化。在这种发展趋势下，外语理所当然地成为人类进入21世纪的通行证，是人类促进和平、繁荣经济、发展科技的重要工具。

一

　　全国第一批外国语学校诞生于1963年。随着我国改革开放的深入发展，全国各地先后办起了不同类型的外国语学校。外国语学校的诞生，为我国外语人才的培养、为我国经济建设的发展作出了积极的贡献。

　　外国语学校是具有专业性教育的学校。它以外语教学为特色，同时全面发展中学的其他学科。"外国语学校的英语教学是中学英语教学的最高层次，是我国英语教学的领头羊。"社会上广泛使用的《看、听、学》（3L系列教材）、《新概念英语》、《展望未来英语教程》等教材都是首先在外国语学校试用后逐步走向社会的。毋庸置疑，在党和政府的关心、指导下，在广大人民群众的理解和支持下，全国外国语学校过去办学的历史是辉煌的。形势的发展，社会的进步，呼唤外国语学校必须要有一套教学理念新颖、教学内容丰富、教学手段创新、适合我国国情的英语教材。为此，全国外国语学校工作理事会在1999年通过决议：集中全国外国语学校的精兵强将，依托全国外国语学校丰富的英语教学经验，编写出一套符合我国外国语学校（包括重点中学）英语教学情况的英语系列教材，使外国语学校在外语教学方面真正起到示范性、辐射性的作用，不辜负国家教育部、各地政府、广大人民群众对外国语学校寄予的殷切希望。通过数年的努力，《英语（全国外国语学校系列教材）》初中教材已全部编写完成并出版，得到了英语教学专家的一致肯定和使用师生的热烈欢迎，并且也顺利通过了教育部的审定。现在，《英语（全国外国语学校系列教材）》高中教材正式出版了。

二

　　《英语（全国外国语学校系列教材）》高中教材以教育部普通高中《英语课程标准》为依据，参照全国外国语学校2000年通过的英语教学大纲，吸收了听说法、情景法、交际法、视听法、结构功能法、主题教学法等诸家教学法的优点，突出"以学生为本"、"以能力为主"的理念，旨在提高学生学习外语的兴趣，增强学生跨文化交流沟通的能力，为培养复合型、应用型、涉外型的高级专门人才奠定坚实的基础。

《英语(全国外国语学校系列教材)》高中教材包括"必修"、"顺序选修"、"任意选修"三个系列，并配有教师用书、练习册和音带。

《英语(全国外国语学校系列教材)》语言纯正地道、内容丰富多彩、编排科学合理，有利于学生进行各项基本训练；注意培养学生听、说、读、写的能力，将思想性、实用性、趣味性和时代性融为一体，使学生在学好英语的同时，在文化修养、思想道德上也有一定的提高。

《英语(全国外国语学校系列教材)》在语言上对学生提出了三方面要求：

1. 语音。语调规范，语感好；能熟练地运用基本的拼读规则和音标读出生词；熟悉英音与美音的基本区别；了解并基本掌握代表不同词义和感情色彩的语调、句子重音变化。

2. 语法。基本掌握英语词法、句法；基本掌握各种英语语法规则，能正确运用语法规则进行口头交流和书面表达。

3. 词汇。初中阶段基本词汇 2 000～2 500 左右，高中阶段基本词汇 3 000～3 500 左右。初、高中阶段的整体认知词汇 9 000 左右（包括基本词汇 5 000～6 000 左右）。

《英语(全国外国语学校系列教材)》对教师也提出了三方面的要求：

1. 语言教学应与文化背景、国情知识介绍相结合。教师在进行语言教学时，应训练学生对课文的整体理解（大部分课文来源于英美国家的原文），注意语言在具体语境中的正确运用；要向学生介绍有关国家的文化背景、风土人情，使学生加深对语言的理解，从而能正确运用语言。

2. 充分调动学生的学习主动性和积极性。各教程都注意留出了一定的思考和实践的空间让学生参与学习，自行完成学习任务。教师在进行语言教学时，要根据教程的要求，结合具体的教学情况，创造良好的语言环境，使学生在轻松愉快的气氛中学到语言、学到知识，增强语言交际的能力，使学生的智力因素和非智力因素得到协调发展。

3. 利用多媒体等现代教学手段，提高语言教学质量。各教程要求教师在教学中能运用现代化的教学手段，使教学变得生动、形象、直观；利用影视声像等营造逼真的语言环境，作用于学生的视觉、听觉，最大限度地调动学生的学习积极性。为适应教学需要，《英语(全国外国语学校系列教材)》编委会和上海外语教育出版社将共同努力，编辑出版与各教程教学有关的视听资料。

武汉外国语学校校长、英语特级教师燕华兴担任高中教材必修、顺序选修系列的主编。

上海外国语大学教授、博士生导师虞建华担任高中教材任意选修系列的主编。

全国一些知名外国语学校的校长、英语教学专家担任《英语(全国外国语学校系列教材)》的编委，或各分册的主编和编委。

上海外国语大学校长、教育部高等学校外语专业教学指导委员会主任委员、博士生导师戴炜栋教授担任《英语(全国外国语学校系列教材)》的总主编，因此本系列教材不仅具有广泛性，更具有权威性。

三

《英语(全国外国语学校系列教材)》的适用对象:

1. 有较高英语教学质量的外国语学校;

2. 有较高英语教学质量的重点中学;

3. 有较高英语教学质量的外语特色学校、双语学校。

外语教学是不断向前发展的，从这个意义而言，《英语(全国外国语学校系列教材)》错误在所难免。如有疏漏、不当之处，欢迎批评指正。希望《英语(全国外国语学校系列教材)》在教学实践中逐步走向成熟。

上海外国语大学党委书记
教授、博士生导师　　　　　　　　　　吴友富
全国外国语学校工作研究会理事长

"任意选修课系列"序言

教育部制定的《普通高中英语课程标准》指出："高中阶段的外语教育是培养公民外语素质的重要过程，它既要满足学生心智和情感态度的发展需求以及高中毕业生就业、升学和未来生存发展的需要，同时还要满足国家的经济建设和科技发展对人才培养的需求。"《标准》同时希望"建立新的外语教育教学理念，使课程设置和课程内容具有时代性、基础性和选择性；建立灵活的课程目标体系，使之对不同阶段和不同地区的英语教学更具有指导意义；建立多元、开放的英语课程评价体系，使评价真正成为教学的有机组成部分；建立规范的英语教材体系以及丰富的课程资源体系，以保障英语课程的顺利实施。"《标准》高屋建瓴，为高中英语教学的改革和发展指明了方向。

正是本着这样的精神，并按照《标准》中提出的有关在高中英语教学设立选修课的具体课程设计思路，我们编写了这套具有时代性、基础性和选择性的"任意选修课系列"，作为新推出的《英语（全国外国语学校系列教材）》高中教材的一部分。本系列包括《初级英语语法与修辞》、《英汉初级笔译》、《英语应用文写作》、《英语报刊阅读》、《英语演讲与辩论》、《文秘英语》、《科技英语》、《初级旅游英语》、《初级经贸英语》、《英美文学欣赏入门》、《英语影视欣赏入门》、《英语戏剧与表演入门》、《英语歌曲欣赏》和《信息技术英语》共14种，旨在为全国外国语学校和省市重点高中的英语教学提供丰富的选修课教材，为发展学生的专业兴趣投石问路，为进入高校后进一步学习深造打好基础，为将来的就业做好铺垫，同时希望这些课程的引入能开阔学生的视野、丰富学生的文化生活。

这套"任意选修课系列"教材是比较超前的，我们设想的使用对象是外语教学处于领先地位和具有外语教学特色的学校。让高中生直接涉及与英语相关的专业学习，最令人担心的是他们的语言能力是否足以应对。我们在编写的过程中充分注意到了这个问题，以"方便操作，引领入门"为原则，充分尊重英语学习的规律，注意课文选择的合理性，注意排除语言障碍，使课文语言通顺易懂，做到既涉及专业知识，又提高语言技能，两者相得益彰。本系列选修教材的编者以著名大学的教授、副教授为主，由他们为高中生编撰实用、简易、易于普及的、与英语相关的专业丛书，并配以简便实用、内容详尽的教师用书，其特点如下：

1. 以国内外国语学校和省市重点高中为使用对象，难度略高于一般的高中教材，适用于英语教学处于较前沿的学校。

2. 注重进一步提高学生的英语理解和表达能力，拓展表达范围。

3. 尽量避免过多的专业词汇和术语，尽量向日常普通英语靠拢，在一些专业性较强的部分，配以汉语解释和其他辅助手段。

4. 注重思想性、趣味性、多样性、可读性，图文并茂，创造轻松、高效学习的必要条件。

5. 以专业入门为原则，以语言教学为重点。

6. 课文后配有注释和练习，以达到复习巩固的目的；在专业方面，练习以认识、了解和初步掌握为目的，对学生不提更高的要求。

在本系列教材的编写过程中，我们要特别感谢上海外国语大学领导的大力支持，也要特别感谢上海外语教育出版社的精心策划、编辑与审定和各方面的有效协调、通力合作。为高中生编撰选修读本是我们的新尝试，不当之处在所难免，敬请批评指正。

虞建华
2005 年 5 月于上海外国语大学

编者的话

用英语表演戏剧，是使外语学习生动有趣而富有成效的途径。现在有不少英语教师也意识到了这一点，把英语短剧表演作为课堂教学的重要辅助手段。但在实际教学中，老师和学生们往往会遇到一些困难。首先是缺乏既适合高中生英语水平、又符合高中生心理特点的剧本，无法满足学生学习英语与陶冶情操的双重需要；二是缺乏西方戏剧基础知识的介绍，致使学生在阅读和欣赏剧本时产生生疏感；三是缺乏对戏剧基本表演技巧的了解，导致表演效果和课堂气氛经常达不到期待值。本书的编写正是为了弥补以上缺憾，希望为热爱英语、热爱戏剧的师生们提供一个有益的教学平台。

本教材供一学期使用，共八个单元。每个单元主要分为四大版块：

第一是戏剧知识介绍（LEARNING SOMETHING ABOUT DRAMA），分为两部分：一是戏剧知识介绍（A CARD ABOUT DRAMA）。戏剧作为一门既独立又综合的艺术，内容可谓广博精深。本书尽量顾及高中生的学习需要，撷取了戏剧中的基本常识加以简要介绍，并配有生动形象的图片帮助学生理解戏剧的特点。二是戏剧知识练习（TRY BY YOURSELF）。本书设计了一些能让学生发挥想像力的练习，使学生在积极思维的过程中加深对戏剧的了解。教师可根据教师用书上的补充信息对相关戏剧知识进行进一步的介绍，也可引导学生自己作相关知识的收集工作。

第二是剧本学习，主要包括预习（PREPARATION）、剧本（SCRIPT）和复习（REFLECTIONS AND DISCUSSIONS）三部分。本教材的剧本都取材于戏剧名家的名段或文学大师的名篇，根据高中生的理解能力和英语水平，在内容上和语言上都进行了相应的改编。在这一版块内配有形式多样、难易有别的练习，便于教师和学生对学习效果进行检测。

第三是戏剧表演技巧简介（A TIP FOR PERFORMANCE）。虽说表演并无定律，但学生必须掌握基本的表演规律，才能准确地传情达意。由于表演有具有相当大的灵活性，所以希望教师在实践中针对学生的个人特点进行指导，并组织好排练和表演过程。

第四是课外练习（HOMEWORK）。这一部分内容是为对戏剧有浓厚兴趣的同学设计的，让他们有更多的机会锻炼自己的表演才能，并提高英语口语的表达能力。教师可根据教学的时间和需要灵活安排这一部分的内容。

本教材的教师用书提供以下内容:

对学生用书内涉及的戏剧知识进行进一步的深入介绍,并提供戏剧知识练习的答案。

对学生用书内课文所涉及的原剧本或文学作品进行内容介绍,介绍课文内的生词的用法,并提供课文的中文译文和配套练习题的参考答案。

为高中生编写英语戏剧欣赏与表演的教材,对编者来说是一次有意义的尝试,也是一次挑战。由于水平有限,疏漏之处在所难免,敬请使用本教材的广大师生批评指正。

编者

2006 年 3 月 8 日

Contents

Pygmalion

I. Learning something about drama

1. A card about drama

(additional information)

A brief history of Western drama

By the 5th century B.C., there arose in the West a spectacular theatre in Athens(雅典). Athenian drama created the forms of both tragedy and comedy, and laid the foundation not only for future Western drama, but also for continuing debates as to how and to what purpose life should be lived.

希腊罗马时期的戏剧　　Greek and Roman Drama: Greek civilization, because of the internal wars, had lost its leading edge by the end of the 5th century B.C., and the power balance shifted to the growing Roman Empire. Excelling in architecture and engineering, the Romans created some astonishing stage buildings. Roman dramatists, however, almost always drew upon Greek sources for their work, and most Roman plays are about Greek characters and Greek struggles.

中世纪时期的戏剧　　Medieval Drama: The fall of Rome (around the 5th century A.D.) brought to an end the classical era of theatre. And when Western drama reappeared shortly before the year 1000, it was an altogether different product, sponsored by the Christian Church, and most of the plays in this period were of religious subjects.

文艺复兴时期的戏剧　　Renaissance Drama: The Renaissance began in Italy in the 14th century (and lasted to the 16th century), when ancient culture was reborn. It was in England that the Renaissance brought forth the greatest dramatic masterpieces of that era, in the works of William Shakespeare.

古典主义时期的戏剧　The Royal Theatre: The Renaissance was followed by an era, which was marked by science and rationality, and politically by the increasing importance of European Royalty. Rational sensibility(理性) dominated the times.

浪漫主义时期的戏剧　The Romantic Theatre: The romantic theatre in the 18th and 19th century was a bold rejection of the rational royal theatre. Romanticism was characterized with the free-flowing spirit of the individual rather than the social organization of class, court, or scientific academy.

现代戏剧　The Modern Drama: The modern drama had its roots deep in the social, political and intellectual revolutions in the 18th and 19th century. Ever since its outset it has been a theatre of challenge, a theatre of experimentation. It has never been a theatre of rules or simple messages, nor has it been a theatre of absolute heroes and villains. The theatre of realism, naturalism, symbolism(象征主义), expressionism(表现主义), the theatre of the Absurd(荒诞派戏剧) and various theatrical movements carried out by the dramatic artists make the modern theatre go on as one of the greatest periods in theatre history.

2. Try by yourself

The components of a play

The six components of a play are arranged in the following order of importance: plot, character, theme, diction, music and spectacle.

(additional information)

Plot(情节) is a structure of actions — both outer actions (such as character A stabs character B) and inner actions (such as character C falls in love with character D).

Characters(人物) are the human figures who undertake the actions of the plot. The fundamental demand of a play's characters is that they make audience care. To this end, characters should be alive with feelings of real people.

Theme(主题) is the play's overall statement: its topic, central idea, or message.

Diction(用语) relates to the pronunciation of spoken dialogue; to the literary character of a play's text, including its tone, imagery, cadence, and articulation; and to its use of literary forms and figures such as verse, rhyme, metaphor, and so on.

Music(音乐) can take different forms. A play may use music in the form of songs and background music. One important function of music is its effectiveness in moving an audience to ever-deeper feeling.

Spectacle(场景) includes the visual aspects of production: scenery, costumes, lighting, makeup, properties, and the overall look of the theatre and stage.

II. Preparation for learning

1. Questions to think about

Do you think proper manners and speech are important for a person's career? Why?

Manners and speech are very important for a person's career, especially those careers that deal with public relations, because if a person cannot speak and behave properly, he will probably be regarded as poorly educated, incompetent or even unfriendly. And an ill-mannered person does not know how to deal with other people within the social rules, so he will not only displease those around him, but also be likely to bring trouble to them and himself. Since cooperation is always required in carrying out a task in today's society, proper manners and speech are extremely important. At the same time, we should take other important factors into consideration when we judge a person, such as his competence, personality and performance. To sum up, the importance of proper manners and speech should neither be understated nor overstated.

2. The whole story of the play

This play is the masterpiece of the English playwright Bernard Shaw. Two old gentlemen meet in the rain one night at Covent Garden. Professor Higgins is a researcher of phonetics, and Colonel Pickering is a linguist of Indian dialects. Higgins bets Pickering that he can, with his knowledge of phonetics, convince high London society that, during a few months, he will be able to transform a flower girl, Eliza Doolittle, into a lady like a duchess. Higgins starts by having his housekeeper bathe Eliza and give her new clothes. For a number of months, Higgins trains Eliza to speak properly. Mrs. Higgins worries that the experiment will lead to problems once it is ended, but Higgins and Pickering are too absorbed in their game to care about her warning. At an ambassador's party, Eliza is a great success. But Higgins and Pickering are now bored with the project, which hurts Eliza greatly. She throws Higgins's slippers at him in a rage because she does not know what is to become of her. He suggests she marry somebody. She returns him the hired jewelry, and he accuses her of ingratitude.

The following morning, Higgins rushes to his mother in a panic because Eliza has run away. Mrs. Higgins, who has been hiding Eliza upstairs all along, chides（嘲笑）the two of them for playing with the girl's affections. When she enters, Eliza thanks Pickering for always treating her as a lady, but threatens Higgins that she will go work with his rival phonetician, Nepommuck. The outraged Higgins cannot help but start to admire her. As Eliza leaves for her father's wedding, Higgins shouts out a few errands（差使）for her to run, assuming that she will return to him at Wimpole Street. Eliza never makes it clear whether she will or not.

NOTE

Pygmalion derives its name from the famous story in Ovid's *Metamorphoses*《变形记》in which Pygmalion, disgusted by the loose and shameful lives of the women of his era, decides to live alone and remain unmarried. With wondrous art, he creates a beautiful statue more perfect than any living woman. The more he looks upon her, the more deeply he falls in love with her, until he wishes that she were more than a statue. This statue is Galatea. Lovesick, Pygmalion goes to the temple of the goddess Venus and prays that she give him a lover like his statue; Venus is touched by his love and brings Galatea to life. When Pygmalion returns from Venus's temple and kisses his statue, he is delighted to find that she is warm and soft to the touch. The maiden feels the kisses, blushes and, lifting her timid eyes up to the light, sees the sky and her lover at the same time.

3. Words and expressions

■ **dialect**
He can speak Shanghai dialect.
他会说上海话。

■ **bet**
He put his bet on that horse.
他把赌注押在那匹马上。

■ **gulf**
The quarrel left a gulf between the old friends.
那场争吵在老友中造成了极深的隔阂。

- **separate**

  The two towns are separated by a river.

  这两个城镇被一条小河隔开了。

- **assure**

  She assured me that she would come.

  她向我保证她一定来。

- **dress**

  He is dressed in old clothes.

  他穿着旧衣服。

- **afterwards**

  She stayed for a while afterwards.

  她后来又待了一会儿。

- **advantage**

  The only advantage of the plan is its simplicity.

  这项计划的唯一优点就是简单易行。

- **manners**

  It wasn't good manners to make too many inquiries into other people's affairs.

  过多地打听别人的事情是不礼貌的。

- **pick up**

  He picked up a lot of information about it.

  他获得了许多关于此事的消息。

- **as to**

  I have no doubts as to your ability.

  对于你的能力我毫不怀疑。

- **pass off**

  She tried passing her husband's work off as her own.

  她试图把她丈夫的作品冒充成自己的。

- **make for**

  It's late. We'd better make for home.

  时间不早了，我们最好赶回家。

卖花女

第三幕（简写版）

人物：
希金斯夫人：希金斯的母亲
亨利·希金斯：语音学教授
皮克林：研究印度方言的语言学家

场景：
在希金斯夫人的客厅。时间是下午4点至5点之间。
门被打开了。希金斯戴着帽子走了进来，皮克林跟在后面。

希金斯夫人：亨利！我没想到你会这个时候回家。

希金斯：母亲，这是我的朋友皮克林。

希金斯夫人：很高兴见到你，皮克林。

皮克林：我很高兴见到您，希金斯夫人。

希金斯夫人：请坐下，皮克林。

皮克林：谢谢。

希金斯（兴奋地）：母亲，我有很重要的事情告诉你！

希金斯夫人：什么事让你这么兴奋？

希金斯：我找了一个姑娘。

希金斯夫人：这是否意味着有个姑娘找了你？

希金斯：根本不是那回事。这跟恋爱无关。

希金斯夫人：那就太遗憾了！

希金斯：她马上就会来见你。

希金斯夫人：我不记得曾经邀请过她。

希金斯：你没有邀请过她。是我邀请的。她是个普通的卖花女。我是在路边找的。

希金斯夫人：然后就邀请她到我家里来？

希金斯（站起身来哄她）：噢，不会有什么不妥的。我已经教会她怎么恰当地说话，她的行为也有严格的规范。

希金斯夫人：天！你怎么可以做这种傻事，亨利？

希金斯：皮克林也参与了这件事。我打了个赌，保证能让她在6个月内变成个淑女。几个月前我就着手做这事了。她的进步神速。我会赢得这个赌注的。她听力敏锐，比我那些中产阶级的学生好教多了。

希金斯夫人：你们两个简直就是在做儿戏，用活人当玩具。

希金斯：儿戏！这是我接手过的最困难的工作。母亲，你可别搞错了。但你无法理解这是件多么有趣的事。通过教一个人一种新的说话方式，把她变成完全不同的另一个人。这会填补阶级与阶级、心灵与心灵之间的鸿沟。

皮克林（把椅子向希金斯夫人拉近一些）：是的，这有趣极了。我可以向你保证。我们对她很当真。每周——几乎每天——

都会有新的变化。

希金斯：是的，这是我做过的最有趣的实验。她充实了我们的生活，是吗，皮克林？

皮克林：我们总是谈论伊丽莎。

希金斯：教导伊丽莎。

皮克林：打扮伊丽莎。

希金斯夫人：什么？

皮克林：创造新的伊丽莎。

希金斯：那个女孩是个天才。她能弹一手漂亮的钢琴。我们已经带她去了古典音乐会和音乐厅。

希金斯夫人：安静，亨利。皮克林，难道你们没有意识到你们有个巨大的问题需要解决吗？

希金斯(不耐烦地)：但有什么问题呢？

希金斯夫人：这事完了以后她怎么办？

希金斯：我不觉得这是个问题。她可以有她自己的生活，我们已经给了她这些优势了。

希金斯夫人：让她就靠礼仪和说话来谋生，而不给她一个淑女的收入？你是这个意思吗？

皮克林(显得挺烦闷地)：噢，这不会有什么麻烦的，希金斯夫人。(他站起身来准备走。)

希金斯(也站起身来)：我们会给她找个工作。

皮克林：她已经够快乐了。你不必为她担心。再见。(他朝门口走去。)

希金斯：不管怎么样，现在不必为此操心。这件事已经做了。再见，母亲。(他尾随皮克林而去。)

IV. Reflections and discussions

1. Write a summary of the script by filling in the blanks with the given words.

---

behave   duchess   absorbing   advantages   pass   bet

Higgins and Pickering told Mrs. Higgins about their _bet_ that they would _pass_ Eliza Doolittle, a common flower girl, as a _duchess_ in six months. Higgins said he had picked her up in the street, and had taught her how to speak and _behave_ properly. Their plan went on smoothly because the girl was quick to learn. They thought they were doing the most _absorbing_ experiment with the girl and the girl would go her own way with all the _advantages_ they had given her, but Mrs. Higgins thought the two treated the girl like a live doll and the girl would find trouble in earning her living in the future. However, the two men paid no attention to her warning and took their leave.

2. True or false

1) Higgins was excited because he had something important to tell his mother. **(T)**

2) Higgins told his mother that he had fallen in love with a girl. **(F)**

3) Higgins taught the girl to speak and behave properly. **(T)**

4) Mrs. Higgins thought their experiment would lead to problems once it was over. **(T)**

5) Higgins thought the experiment with the flower girl was very interesting. **(T)**

3. Multiple choice

1) What was the bet between Higgins and Pickering?

    A. <u>Higgins would change the flower girl into a duchess-like lady in six months.</u>

    B. Higgins would write a book about language and behavior differences.

    C. Higgins would find a good job for the flower girl in six months.

2) Why were Higgins and Pickering excited?

    A. Because they found Eliza was the only genius they had ever seen.

    B. <u>Because they thought what they were doing was an interesting experiment.</u>

    C. Because they thought Eliza would live a better life in the future.

3) What was the difficult problem to solve for Higgins and Pickering?

    A. <u>Eliza couldn't live a good life in the future with the advantages they gave her.</u>

    B. Eliza couldn't feel happy if she was left alone in the future.

    C. Eliza couldn't find anybody else to teach her in the future.

4) What did Higgins and Pickering do in order to pass Eliza off as a fine lady?

    A. <u>They taught her good speech.</u>

    B. They asked her to do experiments every day.

    C. They gave her a good job.

5) Which statement is true about Eliza?

    A. She was quick at everything.

    B. She could play many musical instruments.

    C. <u>She was good at learning language.</u>

4. Questions for discussion

1) Higgins believed that learning good speech and manners could fill up the gulf that separated class from class and soul from soul. Do you agree with his view?

Some people agree with Higgins's point of view. They believe that speech and manners is the first thing to reveal one's social background, educational level and personal characteristics, so if a person can speak and behave elegantly, he or she will be treated as a promising one and be given more and better opportunities for development and will keep going uphill in his or her career. However, other people hold that good speech and manners are only superficial things, and are far from enough to prove one's worth and ability, and may not necessarily lead one to success. One's willingness to learn, one's determination to fulfill his or her goals, and one's capacity in his work is far more important in deciding one's social status.

2) Do you think Eliza would live a better life when she learned how to speak and behave like a duchess?

There are two possible opinions for this question. The first opinion holds that Eliza would live a better and happier life when she was transformed into a lady with excellent speech and manners. She would have more chances to get in touch with the rich or important persons, who might help her to find a good job or even a good husband. The second opinion believes that Eliza wouldn't feel happier. Although she could change her manners and speech, she couldn't change her temperament and habits, and it would be difficult for her to get used to the conventions and customs of the upper-class society. In addition, it would be extremely difficult for her to live as a lady without a sufficient income. That is to say, she would belong to neither the working class nor the middle class, which would be a tragedy for her.

V. A tip for performance

（略）

VI. Self-assessment

（略）

VII. Homework

（略）

Unit Two

Jane Eyre

I. Learning something about drama

1. A card about drama

(additional information)

> A soliloquy is an expanded and developed speech in which a dramatic character speaks his thoughts out loud, for the audience alone. The soliloquy is delivered by the speaker alone on the stage.
>
> An aside is a similar device — though much shorter, often only a single observation, perhaps even just one word. An aside is a "stage whisper" by one character to the audience, while other characters present on stage engage in their own dialogue and movement at the same time.
>
> The devices represent attempts by the dramatists to offer the deeper, inner thoughts of a character. In *Hamlet*, the entire progress of the main characters' constant moral and psychological dilemma is expressed in a series of soliloquies. A character will use a soliloquy when most distressed, confused, scheming or optimistic. In other words, the soliloquy offers deep insights into a character at times of greatest stress, tension, concentration, yearning or suffering. The aside is shorter and lighter, and is more suited to comedy than tragedy.

2. Try by yourself

1) A distant sound is heard, coming as if out of the sky, like the sound of a string snapping, slowly and sadly dying away. (sound cues)

2) The sitting-room at the Ollivants' in a small town. It is an evening late in the spring. (place and time)

3) Old furniture and two woodcuts on the walls create the atmosphere of the past. (general impressions of the place or environment)

4) Mary, a rather plain woman of about 25, is standing, lost in thought, looking out into the garden. (age and physical action of the character)

(additional information)

Character Stage Directions are placed directly under the character's name or between the lines of dialogue of a single speech. Most playwrights use this kind of stage directions sparingly.

- Physical action to be done as the line is being spoken: (Filling the glass)
- Action implying the equivalent of a pause: (Shaking her head)
- Tone of voice or emotional quality of the line: (Distraught)
- Clarifying who the line is said to when more than two characters are on stage: (To Joan)

General Stage Directions within Acts or Scenes stand alone in the manuscript. They're singly spaced and usually deal with physical action or a combination of physical action and lighting or sound effects.

II. Preparation for learning

1. Questions to think about

What are the personal characteristics that an ideal marriage partner must possess? Do you have some of them?

There are many admirable qualities an ideal marriage partner may possess: honesty, independence, modesty, loyalty, patience, humor, gentleness, good nature, tidiness, a broad mind, good manners, diligence, ambition, generosity, and so on. But first of all, an ideal marriage requires that a man and woman love each other, understand each other and tolerate each other's defects.

2. The whole story of the play

Jane Eyre is the masterpiece of the 19th century English novelist Charlotte Bronte. Jane Eyre is a young orphan raised by Mrs. Reed, her cruel, wealthy aunt. When she is sent off to a school at Lowood, she suffers a lot from the cold-blooded headmaster. Later, Jane is employed as a governess at a manor called Thornfield for a little girl, Adèle. After much waiting, Jane finally meets her employer, Edward Rochester, a man who seems to have a dark past. Other oddities around Thornfield include the occasional strange and frightening laugh Jane hears from the third-story attic(阁楼). Meanwhile, Jane develops a secret love for Rochester. However, Jane feels depressed when Rochester brings home a beautiful but vicious woman named Blanche Ingram. Jane believes that Rochester will propose to Miss Ingram. Rochester explains that he is well aware that it is his money instead of himself that Miss Ingram loves, and he asks Jane to marry him, instead. Jane accepts, but a month later, their wedding ceremony is interrupted because it is made known to Jane that Rochester already has a wife called Bertha, a lunatic(疯子) kept in the attic in Thornfield. Rochester confesses his past misdeeds to Jane. In his youth he married the wealthy Bertha for money, but was unaware of her family's history of hereditary(遗传性的) madness, and over time she became such a dangerous woman that nothing but the imprisonment could stop her from making mischief. Despite his protests that he loves Jane, she cannot agree to marry him because of his previous marriage, and leaves Thornfield. Penniless and hungry, Jane is forced to sleep outdoors and beg for food. At last, three siblings(兄弟姐妹) take her in. Their names are Mary, Diana, and St. John Rivers, and Jane quickly becomes a close friend to them. St. John is a clergyman(牧师), and he finds Jane a job teaching at a charity(慈善) school. He surprises her one day by declaring that her uncle, John Eyre, has died and left her a large fortune: 20,000 pounds. When Jane asks how he has received this news, he shocks her further by declaring that her uncle was also his uncle: Jane and the Riverses are cousins. Jane immediately decides to share her inheritance equally with her three newfound relatives. St. John decides to travel to India as a missionary(传教士), and he urges Jane to accompany him — as his wife. Jane agrees to go to India but refuses to marry him because she does not love him. Jane later returns to Thornfield and finds that it has been burned to the ground by Bertha Mason, who lost her life in the fire. Rochester saved the servants but lost his eyesight and one of his hands. Jane travels on to Rochester's new residence, and they resume their relationship and get married soon. At the end of her story, Jane writes that she has been married for ten blissful(无忧的) years and that she and Rochester enjoy perfect equality in their life together. She says that after two years of blindness, Rochester regained sight in one eye and was able to behold their first son at his birth.

3. Words and expressions

- **plain**

  She was neither quite pretty nor quite plain.

  她既不美，也不难看。

- **gift**

  He was gifted with dramatic power.

  他有演戏的天赋。

- **equal**

  The two are equal in ability. (*adj.*)

  这两个人能力差不多。

  Make friends with your equals or betters. (*n.*)

  与同你相仿或更好的人做朋友。

- **offer**

  He offered her a cigarette.

  他主动给了她一支香烟。

- **share**

  They divided the money into equal shares.

  他们把钱分成了相等的几份。

- **self**

  He put his whole self into the job.

  他把全部身心都投入到工作中去了。

- **intend**

  They intend to publish the novel in France.

  他们打算在法国出版这本小说。

- **doubt**

  I doubt whether we shall succeed.

  我怀疑我们是否能成功。

- **cause**

  These problems are caused by increasing unemployment.

  这些问题是因为失业人数不断增加造成的。

- **rumor**

  Various rumors about him are going around.

  到处流传着关于他的种种谣言。

- **swear**

  Will you swear that you were not there?

  你愿意起誓说你当时不在场吗?

- **run into**

  I run into my English teacher in the street yesterday.

  我昨天在街上偶然遇到了我的英语老师。

III. Script

简·爱

人物:

简·爱: 桑菲尔德庄园的家庭女教师,相貌平常

爱德华·罗切斯特: 桑菲尔德庄园的主人

场景:

傍晚。简在花园的小路上遇见了罗切斯特。

简: 离开桑菲尔德我感到痛苦。我爱桑菲尔德,因为我在这里过着丰富、愉快的生活,至少在这短暂的时间里是这样。但现在我认为我必须离开了。

罗切斯特: 你为什么这么想?

简: 是你让我这么想的。我知道高贵美丽的英格拉姆小姐将成为你的新娘。

罗切斯特: 我的新娘!什么新娘?我没有新娘。

简: 可是你会有的。

罗切斯特: 对,我会有!我会有!(他咬紧牙齿)

简: 你都已经亲口说了。那我得走了。

罗切斯特: 不,你得留下!

简: 我告诉你我必须走!你以为我是一个没有感情的物体吗?你以为,因为我出身贫穷、身份低微、相貌平庸、身材矮小,我就没有灵魂,没有心灵吗?你想错了!如果上帝赐予我一点美貌和财富,我就要让你感到难以离开我,就像我现在难以离开你一样。现在我的精神在同你的精神说话,就像我们两个人都经过了坟墓,站在上帝的脚跟前,是平等的——因为我们是平等的!

罗切斯特：因为我们是平等的！就这样，就这样，简！

简：是的，就这样，先生。我不会留下来成为你觉得无足轻重的人。我要去爱尔兰。我已经把我心里的话说出来了，现在上哪儿都行。

罗切斯特：简，安静点，别这么挣扎，像只发怒的野鸟似的。

简（笔直地站着）：我不是鸟，也没有罗网捕捉我。我是个有独立意志的自由人。

罗切斯特：你的意志将决定你的命运。我把我的手、我的心和我的财产的分享权都奉献给你。

简：别逗我了！

罗切斯特：我要你一辈子都在我身边，做我的第二个自己和最好的人间伴侣。

简：但你已经做出了你的选择，那就是英格拉姆小姐。

罗切斯特：简，你太激动了。到我身边来，让我们做些解释，彼此谅解吧。

简：我永远也不会到你身边去。

罗切斯特：可是，简，我打算娶的只是你。

简：别开玩笑了！

罗切斯特：来吧，简，过来。

简：你的新娘拦在我们中间。

罗切斯特：我的新娘在这里。（把简拉向他）因为我的另一半在这里。简，你愿意嫁给我吗？

简：……

罗切斯特：你怀疑我吗？

简：完全怀疑。

罗切斯特：在你的眼睛里，我是个撒谎者吗？让我解释给你听。我对英格拉姆小姐有什么爱情呢？没有。她对我有什么爱情呢？没有。这是我证实了的：我让一个谣言传到她耳朵里，说我的财产连人家猜想的三分之一都不到。在那以后，我发现她和她母亲都对我非常冷淡。我不会——我也不能——娶英格拉姆小姐。但你，你是我的天使。我真心希望你接受我做你的丈夫。

简：什么，我？在世界上除了你以外——如果你是我的朋友的话——没有一个朋友的我？除了你给我的钱以外没有一个先令的我？

罗切斯特：是的，简。你愿意成为我的吗？说愿意，快。

简：你当真吗？你真的爱我吗？你是真心实意地希望我做你的妻子吗？

罗切斯特：是的。要是必须有一个誓言，那我就起誓。

简：那么，先生，我愿意嫁给你。

罗切斯特：爱德华，我的小妻子！

简：亲爱的爱德华！

罗切斯特：到我这儿来，现在完完全全地到我这儿来。（用低沉的声音）使我幸福吧——我将使你幸福。

IV. Reflections and discussions

1. Write a summary of the script by filling in the blanks with the given words.

> intended   independent   plain   supposed   property   rumor

When Jane mistakenly thought Rochester would marry Miss Ingram, she decided to leave Thornfield for Ireland. She ran into Rochester in the garden, expressed her love to Rochester and showed her _independent_ will in spite of the fact that she was poor and _plain_. Rochester explained to Jane that there was no love between Miss Ingram and him, because after Miss Ingram believed the _rumor_ that his _property_ was much less than what was _supposed_, she became very cold to him. Rochester told Jane it was only her that he _intended_ to marry, and he made a proposal to Jane. When the misunderstanding was got rid of, Jane gave her hand to Rochester.

2. True or false

1) Jane felt sad to leave Thornfield because she lived a happy life there. **(T)**

2) Jane was neither good-looking nor rich. **(T)**

3) Miss Ingram loved Rochester although the fortune of Rochester was not a third of what was supposed. **(F)**

4) It was hard for Jane to leave Rochester. **(T)**

5) Rochester asked Jane to stay with him forever. **(T)**

3. Multiple choice

1) Jane was angry because _____
   A. Rochester had not told her that he would marry Miss Ingram.
   B. she thought she was poor, obscure, plain and little.
   C. she thought Rochester paid no attention to her feelings.

2) Why did Jane decide to go to Ireland?
   A. Because she had a job offer in Ireland.
   B. Because she did not want to stay in Thornfield to become nothing to Rochester.
   C. Because she thought Ireland was a good place to live in.

3) What did Rochester do to test his relationship with Miss Ingram?
   A. He told a lie about his fortune.
   B. He had a talk with the mother of Miss Ingram.
   C. He played a joke on Miss Ingram.

4) Why did Rochester say he couldn't marry Miss Ingram?

    A. Because someone caused a rumor which harmed their relationship.

    B. Because Miss Ingram's mother didn't like Rochester.

    C. <u>Because what Miss Ingram loved was Rochester's money.</u>

5) Why did Rochester love Jane?

    A. <u>Jane was independent and self-respecting.</u>

    B. Jane was plain and little.

    C. Jane was gifted with much wealth.

4. Questions for discussion

1) What kind of girl was Jane?

According to Jane herself, she was poor, obscure, plain and little. However, we can find some admirable qualities in this girl.

She was sincere in her love for Rochester. She loved Rochester and expressed her feelings rather directly. Although she realized she was not beautiful or rich, she believed everyone was equal to love and to be loved.

She was independent. When she thought Rochester would marry Miss Ingram, she decided to leave and have a new life in Ireland, although she could choose to stay and get the payment from Rochester like before.

She had high self-respect. Although she had deep love for Rochester, she felt a strong need to be respected by him, and she would not sacrifice her self and dignity for the sake of feelings.

2) If love is based on money, what will be the problems?

If love is based on money, the couple will quarrel with each other very often about monetary matters and no quiet and happy life between them is possible.

If love is based on monetary, the couple cannot really understand or appreciate each other. It is very hard for them to share each other's spiritual enjoyments, which is equally important in one's life. It is also difficult for them to shoulder each other's troubles, especially monetary matters.

If love is based on money, the couple is very likely to break up when they are in financial difficulties or when someone with more money appears.

If love is based on money, the love is not love at all.

V. A tip for performance

（略）

VI. Self-assessment

（略）

VII. Homework

（略）

Hamlet

I. Learning something about drama

1. A card about drama

(additional information)

> A tragedy is a serious play. The central character, often called the protagonist, is a person of high rank. During the play, the protagonist undergoes a decline of fortune, leading to suffering and death. Integral to tragedy is the protagonist's period of insightful recognition or understanding.
>
> Comedy is not a simple amusement, however, nor is comedy simply entertaining; comedy is always about a serious human conflict. The passionate pursuit of love, ambition, social status, and money are age-old themes.
>
> Tragicomedy is a form that deliberately attempts to bridge the two original genres. It maintains a serious theme throughout but varies the approach from serious to humorous. It has been called "tragedy that ends happily."

2. Try by yourself

1) Do you know the famous plays of Shakespeare? Match the pictures with the plays.

   Hamlet (Picture 2), *Romeo and Juliet* (Picture 1), *Merchant of Venice* (Picture 3)

2) Arrange the following facts about Shakespeare according to the order of time.

1	4	2	5	3

(additional information)

William Shakespeare is the most widely admired and respected writer in the English language. However, in his own lifetime, things were different. Although his plays were always popular, Shakespeare was not known as the "greatest" of Elizabethan(伊丽莎白时代的) writers. Perhaps because of this, we find few documents relating to Shakespeare's life.

William Shakespeare's father, John Shakespeare, was a successful landowner, moneylender, and wool and agricultural goods dealer. Not much is known about his childhood, although it is safe to assume that he attended the local grammar school, the King's New School, where many teachers held Oxford degrees. He did not attend the university, but this was not unusual at the time, since university education was reserved for prospective clergymen and was not a particularly mind-opening experience. However, the education he received at the grammar school was excellent, which laid a good foundation for his play writing. More impressive than his formal education is the wealth of general knowledge exhibited in his works, from a working knowledge of many professions to a vocabulary far greater than any other English writer.

In 1582, at age eighteen, William Shakespeare married 26-year-old Anne Hathaway. In about 1589 Shakespeare wrote his first play, *Henry VI, Part 1*. Sometime between his marriage and writing this play he and his wife moved to London, where he pursued a career as a playwright and actor. Acting and writing plays at this time were not considered noble professions, but successful and prosperous actors were relatively well respected. Shakespeare was very successful and made quite a bit of money, which he invested in real estate(房地产).

William Shakespeare lived until 1616. He was buried in the chancel of his church at his hometown Stratford-on-Avon. The lines above his tomb (allegedly written by Shakespeare himself) read:

Good friend, for Jesus' sake forbear

To dig the dust enclosed here.

Blessed be the man that spares these stones

And cursed be he that moves my bones.

II. Preparation for learning

1. Questions to think about

Do you think a prince's life is happier than an ordinary person's? Why or why not?

Some people think a prince's life is happier than an ordinary person's because a prince can enjoy the best food, wear the best clothes, and receive the best education. A prince needn't work hard to earn a living for himself. A prince is always the center of his people's attention, and wherever he goes he is respected. A prince has supreme power over his subjects, and his orders are to be strictly obeyed. But quite on the contrary, an ordinary person keeps worrying about his living all his life. In comparison with a prince, an ordinary person always works more and achieves less.

But some people think a prince's life is not as happy as an ordinary person's. Although he enjoys a lot of privileges in every aspect of his life, he is not given much freedom in deciding what to do. He mustn't violate the numerous rules that are supposed to be observed by a prince; and he must fulfill the duties that are imposed on him by his country and his people. A prince is so important to the whole country that he cannot live a carefree life that an ordinary person can easily enjoy.

2. The whole story of the play

Hamlet is the son of the late King Hamlet of Denmark, who died two months before the start of the play. After King Hamlet's death, his brother, Claudius, becomes king, and marries King Hamlet's widow, Gertrude. At a midnight Hamlet sees with his own eyes the late King Hamlet's ghost, who tells Hamlet privately that Claudius has indeed murdered the King by pouring poison in his ear. Shocked and enraged as he is, Hamlet secretly plans to confirm the story told by the ghost and waits for a chance to revenge his father. In order not to be suspected by Claudius, Hamlet pretends to have lost his mind. He even badly treats his love Ophelia, who is the daughter of Polonius, an advisor of King Claudius, prompting Polonius to believe Hamlet is madly in love with his daughter, though Claudius has doubts. Polonius has allowed his son Laertes to leave for France, and has ordered Ophelia not to have anything to do with Hamlet. Claudius, fearing Hamlet may try to kill him, sends Hamlet to England. Before his leaving, however, Hamlet makes an acting company to reenact King Hamlet's murder before Claudius in the hope of deciding whether the ghost's story is true or not by judging Claudius's reaction. Claudius's enragement and sudden leaving confirm the story of the murder. Hamlet's mother tries to reason with Hamlet after the play, while Polonius spies on them from behind a curtain. Hamlet hears Polonius, and kills him through the curtain, thinking the person is Claudius. After finding out the truth, Hamlet regrets the death. Claudius still sends him to England, accompanied by Rosencrantz and Guildenstern with orders from Claudius that the English kill Hamlet as soon as they arrive.

After Hamlet leaves, Laertes returns from France, and is enraged at Polonius' death.

Ophelia reacts to her father's death with utter madness and eventually falls in a stream and drowns, further angering Laertes. On the way to England, Hamlet finds the orders and changes them to have Rosencrantz and Guildenstern killed, though Hamlet is kidnapped by pirates one day later. The pirates return Hamlet to Claudius for a ransom, and Claudius tries one last attempt to kill Hamlet: he arranges a sword duel between Laertes and Hamlet. The trick, however, is that the tip of Laertes's sword is poisoned. Claudius also poisons the victory cup in case Hamlet wins. During the fight, the poisoned drink is offered to Hamlet, he declines, and instead his mother, Gertrude, drinks it to the objection of Claudius. Laertes, losing to Hamlet, illegally scratches him with the poisoned sword to ensure Hamlet's death. Hamlet unknowingly switches swords with Laertes, and cuts and poisons him. The queen dies, screaming that she has been poisoned and Laertes, dying, admits Claudius's treachery. Weakened as he is, Hamlet stabs Claudius and kills him. Laertes dies, and Hamlet dies after he makes his death speech.

3. Words and expressions

- **revenge**

  He revenged his dead brother.

  他为亡兄报了仇。

- **painful**

  That is a long and painful illness.

  那是一种漫长而痛苦的疾病。

- **shocked**

  He had a shocked expression when he heard the news.

  当他听到这个消息的时候，脸上一副吃惊的表情。

- **sting**

  A bee stung him on the neck.

  一只蜜蜂叮了他的脖子。

- **brief**

  You should make your report brief and to the point.

  你应该使你的报告简单扼要。

- **reveal**

  The doctor did not reveal to him his hopeless condition.

医生没有向他透露说他的病没有治了。

- **gesture**

  He gestured at her to sit.

  他打手势示意她坐下。

- **promise**

  He promised her a quick answer.

  他答应她从速答复。

- **behave**

  He behaved with great courage.

  他表现得非常勇敢。

III. Script

哈姆雷特

第一幕，第五场

人物：

哈姆雷特：丹麦王子

鬼魂：丹麦已故国王，哈姆雷特的父亲

赫拉修：哈姆雷特的朋友

马西勒斯：军人

在高台上。

[鬼魂和哈姆雷特同上]

哈姆雷特：你要把我带到哪里去？回答我——否则我就不走了。

鬼魂（用低沉的声音说）：听我说。

哈姆雷特：我在听。

鬼魂：黎明快来了，我马上就要回到可怕的地狱去。

哈姆雷特：哎，可怜的鬼魂！

鬼魂：不用可怜我。请你仔细地听好我就要告诉你的话。

哈姆雷特：说吧，我必须要知道。

鬼魂：等你听完了，你一定要为我报仇。

哈姆雷特：什么？

鬼魂：我是你父亲的阴魂。听着，啊！

听着！如果你还爱过你的父亲……（鬼魂发出一声惨呼。）

哈姆雷特（震惊地）：天哪！

鬼魂：你就必须为他遭受的谋杀报仇。

哈姆雷特：谋杀！

鬼魂：是的，最残酷、最怪异的谋杀。

哈姆雷特：告诉我发生了什么！

鬼魂：听着，哈姆雷特：他们说，当我在花园里睡着的时候被蛇咬死了。全丹麦人民都被蒙骗了。（停顿）但咬死你父亲的那条毒蛇现在却戴上了他的王冠！

哈姆雷特：我的叔叔！我早就应该想到这一点了！

鬼魂：是的，他是个禽兽！他引诱了你的母亲！噢！哈姆雷特，这是多大的耻辱啊！

哈姆雷特：噢，不！

鬼魂：让我长话短说。当我在花园里睡着时，你的叔叔悄悄走近我，把毒液灌进了我的耳朵里。就这样，我的兄弟的手，让我失去了我的妻子和王位连同我的生命。啊，恐怖！啊，恐怖！真是恐怖之极！（鬼魂仰天呼叫。）如果你爱你的父亲并且拒绝接受这样的罪恶，你就不能容忍高贵的丹麦王君的御床，变成乱伦的场所。（抬头向上看）天快亮了。别了，别了，哈姆雷特。你要记住我。

[鬼魂下]

哈姆雷特：啊，天使啊！啊，大地啊！啊，地狱啊！不要再折磨我了！我可怜的鬼魂，我会记住你的话，为你报谋杀之仇！

[赫拉修与马西勒斯同上。他们朝着王子的方向跑来。]

赫拉修：我的大人，我的大人！

马西勒斯：哈姆雷特大人！

哈姆雷特：喂，喂，我的孩子！

马西勒斯：一切还好吗，我尊贵的大人？

赫拉修：有什么消息，我的大人？告诉我们。

哈姆雷特：我不能说。你们会泄露出去的。

赫拉修：不，我不会，我的大人。我发誓。

马西勒斯：我也不会，我的大人。

哈姆雷特（做手势让他们靠近一点）：丹麦有一个恶棍。

赫拉修：这倒用不着叫鬼魂从坟墓里爬出来告诉我们。

哈姆雷特：当然，一点儿也不错。但刚才所见是一个真正的鬼魂。我不能告诉你们鬼魂与我之间发生的事情。现在，朋友们，请答应我一件事。

赫拉修：我们一定答应。是什么，我的大人？

哈姆雷特：永远也不要说出你们今晚从我这里听到的一切。

赫拉修，马西勒斯：我的大人，我们不会。

哈姆雷特：到这里来，先生们，把你们的手放到我的剑上。凭我的剑起誓，永远也不要说出你们今晚的所闻。

赫拉修，马西勒斯（把他们的手放在哈姆雷特的剑上）：我们凭大人的剑起誓，我们决不泄露今晚发生的一切。

哈姆雷特：好，先生们。以后我的行为和言谈都会变得很古怪，但请你们保持缄默，我请求你们。秩序已经沦丧，我生下来的使命就是要去纠正它！来吧，我们一起走吧！

IV. Reflections and discussions

1. Write a summary of the script by filling in the blanks with the given words.

murdered	shocked	revenge	reveal	swore	poison

On the battlement, the ghost told Hamlet that he is indeed Hamlet's father and that he was _murdered_. The ghost asked Hamlet to _revenge_ his murder and Hamlet agreed. Hamlet was _shocked_ when the ghost went on to tell him that he was murdered by his own brother, Claudius. Unlike the story that a serpent bit the old king as Claudius told the people in Denmark, the ghost told Hamlet that during his afternoon nap Claudius poured _poison_ in the king's ear. Hamlet was very angry, and _swore_ that he would remember the ghost and what the ghost asked of him. Horatio and Marcellus found him and Hamlet had them swear that they would _reveal_ to no one the events about the ghost. Before the scene ends, Hamlet warns his friends that he will pretend to be crazy until he can revenge his father.

2. True or false

1) The ghost was a friend of Hamlet's father. **(F)**
2) The ghost had to return to the underworld after the dawn. **(F)**
3) All the people in Denmark believed that the old king was killed by his brother. **(F)**
4) The dead king asked Hamlet not to revenge the murder. **(F)**
5) Hamlet would pretend to be mad in the future. **(T)**

3. Multiple choice

1) Which of the following statements is true?
   A. The old king was stung by a snake.
   B. The brother of the old king had a heart as evil as a snake.
   C. The old king was killed by the poison of a snake.

2) The whole Denmark believed that _____
   A. the old king was killed by a snake.
   B. the old king was killed by the poisonous liquid.
   C. the old king was killed by his brother.

3) The ghost said the murder was _____

   A. <u>most cruel and unnatural.</u>

   B. a lie.

   C. believed by the whole Denmark.

4) The ghost asked Hamlet to _____

   A. immediately tell all the people in Denmark about the murder.

   B. <u>revenge the murder.</u>

   C. keep secret the talk between them.

5) What did Hamlet ask Horatio and Marcellus to do?

   A. <u>He asked them to keep secret what happened that night.</u>

   B. He asked them to revenge his father.

   C. He asked them to set right the order of things.

4. Questions for discussion

1) Why did Hamlet ask his friends to keep secret what happened that night?

   Because the murder of Hamlet's father had not been proved by any solid evidence, Hamlet had to wait for some time to gather evidence. What's more, his uncle was the king and had power. If his friends revealed what happened that night, Hamlet would have no chance to prove the truth and his life would be in danger.

2) In contemporary time when few people believe the existence of a ghost any more, the ghost is still widely used as a character in movies and literature. How can you explain such a phenomenon?

   The presence of a ghost can always make a movie or a novel more interesting and exciting, and consequently make a movie or a novel popular, which is very important for a movie producer or a novelist. The ghost in a movie or a novel can also be explained psychologically because some psychologists believe that ghost in a story is always a mental construct of the central character. Literary critics sometimes say that ghost is sometimes used in a novel simply because the author cannot tell a complete story without a ghost. As in this drama, nobody except his father himself can tell Hamlet what happens to him. Without knowing his father's murder, no story will be possible.

V. A tip for performance

（略）

VI. Self-assessment

（略）

VII. Homework

（略）

Spectacles

I. Learning something about drama

1. A card about drama

(additional information)

Lighting

Although it is customary to think of theatre lighting as dating from the invention of electricity, nothing can be more misleading. Lighting has always been a major theatrical consideration. The ancient Greeks took best advantage of the sun's rays. The medieval outdoor theatre made use of several devices to redirect sunlight, including halos made of reflective metal to surround the main characters with a focused and intensified light. In the middle ages, lighting technology in indoor stagings became sophisticated. In a 1439 production in Florence, one thousand oil lamps were used for illumination. And by the 16th century, the great festival lighting of indoor theatres would serve as a symbol of the intellectual and artistic achievements of the Renaissance itself. People went to the theatres to revel in light and escape the outside gloom. It was the invention of the gaslight in the 19th century and the development of electricity that brought stage lighting into its modern phase. Electricity provides an enormously flexible form of lighting. The incandescent filament is a reasonably small, cool point of light that can be focused, reflected, aimed, shaped and colored by a great variety of devices; and electric light can be trained in innumerable ways upon actors, scenery, audiences to create realistic or atmospheric effects. Today, thanks to the computer technology, it is not uncommon to see theatres with nearly a thousand lighting instruments all under the complete control of a single technician seated in a comfortable booth above the audience.

Scenery

Modern scenery is generally either realistic or metaphoric — or a combination of both. Realistic scenery attempts to depict, often in great detail, a specific time and place in the real world. Metaphoric scenery favors visual images that seek to suggest the play's intended theme, mood, of social/political implications. Metaphoric scenery tends to remind us — at least when we first see it — that we are in a theatre, not in a bedroom or butcher shop; generally its intention is to draw us more deeply into the play's larger issues and concerns.

2. Try by yourself

Choose the appropriate section on the stage for each of the following dramatic events.

Two persons are quarrelling badly over an important decision.   1

Two friends are chatting over tea.   2

Two persons are discussing serious business.   3

A leader makes a long speech.   4

The girl is standing by the window, looking at the moon, lost in thought.   5

A person loses his senses and makes strange comments.   6

美国耶鲁大学教授亚历山大曾对六个舞台区位作过如下说明：

区位1：由于这个区位处于前舞台中部，因而明显、有力，适合表演紧张的高潮、争吵或重大决定的做出。

区位2：这个区位显出亲切、温暖和非正式的格调，适合于表现家庭之乐、友人品茗聊天、客人拜访、谈情说爱等内容。

区位3：这个区位比区位2正式一点、严肃一点，因而也缺少一点亲切感觉，适合表演社交拜访、公事、阴谋、独白等，无戏的演员也较适宜在此停留。

区位4：这个区位显得正式、高贵，意味着权威，适合表演法庭和法官的宣告、领袖人物发表长篇讲话和展示统治权威。也用于需要特别强调的人物上场。

区位5：这个区位显得浪漫和抒情，适合表演站在窗边凝视天际明月、浪漫的恋爱、梦想和沉思等。

区位6：这是舞台上最弱的区位，但也常常由于违背人们的视觉习惯和心理习惯，反而表现出特殊的力度。例如，这里可以表演杀人、自杀和发疯等。这类过于刺激和粗暴的事件，放在这个最弱的区位来表演可能会雅观一点。

II. Preparation for learning

1. Questions to think about

Why do people need spectacles? What will happen to a poor-sighted person if he does not wear spectacles?

Some people need spectacles because they are poor-sighted, for example, near-sighted or far-sighted. With the help of the glasses, they can see the things as clearly as those who have normal eyesight. Glasses are also commonly used to protect the eyes from the sun, wind, strong light, or dirt. For some, the spectacles are only used as a decoration, that is to say, they wear spectacles simply to appear more beautiful, handsome, or cool. Some uses glasses to cover a scar or something else they think unpleasant to see.

A poor-sighted person without his spectacles will surely have trouble in making a correct judgment about things. The inconvenience caused by the kind of situation ranges from a simple amusement to fatal danger. What we will learn in the text is a case that is both amusing and dangerous. It is quite advisable for those poor-sighted, especially those who have been used to wearing them, to wear their glasses whenever necessary.

2. The whole story of the play

This is a short story written by famous American writer Edgar Allen Poe in 1844. Robert Simpson was a handsome but poor-sighted young man. He refused to wear spectacles because he thought he didn't look good with them. On an opera night he fell in love at first sight with Madame Lalande, whom he believed was the most beautiful woman he had ever seen, and soon made a marriage proposal to her. In order to teach Simpson a lesson, Lalande accepted his proposal, and asked him to put on the spectacles. To his astonishment, Simpson found that Lalande was old enough to be his grandmother. At last Simpson married Lalande's granddaughter as suggested by Madame Lalande, and he never again went without his spectacles.

3. Words and expressions

- **insist**

  He insisted that you were present.
  他坚持说你是在场的。

- **proposal**

  She has had a proposal.

  已经有人向她求婚了。

- **request**

  They made a request that the prisoners should be set free.

  他们要求释放犯人。

- **vanity**

  He did it out of vanity.

  他是出于虚荣心才做这件事情的。

- **confused**

  He felt a little confused about it.

  他对这件事感到有一些困惑。

- **instead**

  He is tired; let me go instead.

  他累了，让我去吧。

- **get over**

  I don't think she ever got over his death.

  我想她一直在为他的死伤心不已。

III. Script

眼 镜

人物：

叙述人

罗伯特·辛普森：一个英俊的年轻人，眼睛近视

拉琅德夫人：一个年老的富有寡妇，年轻时是个美人

斯蒂芬尼·普雷斯顿：拉琅德夫人的孙女，一个可爱漂亮的年轻女孩

叙述人： 罗伯特最后终于说服拉琅德夫人嫁给他。她坚持说自己的年龄比罗伯特大得太多了，但罗伯特说那不要紧。当然，当拉琅德夫人答应了他的求婚时，所

有人都感到非常惊讶。在婚礼的前一夜，罗伯特去看拉琅德夫人。开门的是斯蒂芬尼。

斯蒂芬尼：噢，你好，罗伯特。请进。

辛普森：谢谢，斯蒂芬尼。拉琅德夫人在吗？

斯蒂芬尼：请稍等一会儿。她正在等你。

辛普森：对，我收到了她的便条。她说我必须马上来见她。

斯蒂芬尼：噢，她来了。你们俩单独谈吧。

拉琅德夫人：你好，罗伯特。我知道你收到我的便条了。请坐，亲爱的。我有事必须要告诉你。

辛普森：你看上去神秘兮兮的，亲爱的。怎么了？

拉琅德夫人：别着急。你马上就知道了。在我们结婚之前我有一个请求。前几天你说过你可以为我做任何事。这是个很简单的请求。你会去做我让你做的事情吗？

辛普森：当然，亲爱的。你让我做任何事都行。

拉琅德夫人：那么你把这眼镜戴上吧。

辛普森：眼镜？为什么？我不喜欢眼镜。我从来不戴它。我戴上眼镜难看极了。

拉琅德夫人：请你戴上吧，罗伯特。你答应过我的。（她递给他一副眼镜。）

辛普森：好吧。君子一言，驷马难追。你在干什么？（他戴上了眼镜。）

拉琅德夫人：我把灯都打开。好了。

辛普森（震惊地）：啊！

拉琅德夫人：罗伯特·辛普森，你看清我了吗？

辛普森（踉跄地跌到墙边）：看清了……

拉琅德夫人：你第一次看清了拉琅德夫人！你看到她满脸都是皱纹。你看到她脸上涂着脂粉和口红。你看到了她脱去了让她显得年轻美貌的假发的样子。现在你还说我是世界上最漂亮的女人吗？你还说你想娶我吗？我想不会的，年轻人。我已经老得可以做你的祖母了。你的骄傲和虚荣让你不愿意戴眼镜。如果你早点戴上眼镜，你就会发现我是什么样了。我曾经漂亮过，但现在已经老了。现在我抹上脂粉，戴上假发，看上去样子还过得去。你早该发现我对你来说是太老了。城里的每个人都发现了。罗伯特，亲爱的孩子，我决定给你一个教训。现在，你还有什么可说的？

辛普森（快要晕厥过去）：没什么。我没什么可说的了。我脑子里乱极了。

拉琅德夫人：你是个好孩子，罗伯特。我会一直爱你的，就像一个祖母爱她的孙子一样。你为什么不娶我的孙女呢？可以肯定斯蒂芬尼看上去既年轻又漂亮。即便你戴上眼镜看也是如此。

叙述人：这就是故事的经过。当罗伯特从了解到拉琅德夫人的真相的震惊中恢复以后，他开始追求她的孙女斯蒂芬尼。几个月后，他们结婚了。你可以肯定，他再也离不开他的眼镜了，特别是当他看漂亮女人的时候。

IV. Reflections and discussions

1. Write a summary of the script by filling in the blanks with the given words.

> vanity wig proposal spectacles wedding wrinkles

Simpson made a marriage _proposal_ to Madame Lalande. In order to teach Simpson a lesson, Madame Lalande accepted his proposal, and asked him to put on the _spectacles_ the night before their _wedding_. To his astonishment, Simpson found that Madame Lalande was old enough to be his grandmother: there are many _wrinkles_ on her face, and she wore a _wig_ to make her look young and beautiful. His pride and _vanity_ made him ignore all these facts. At last Simpson married Madame Lalande's granddaughter, and he never again went without his spectacles.

2. True or false

1) Robert decided to marry Madame Lalande when he had already known her very well. **(F)**
2) Robert thought he did not look well in spectacles. **(T)**
3) Robert said he would do anything for Madame Lalande. **(T)**
4) Madame Lalande taught Robert a lesson because she disliked him and wanted to make a fool of him. **(F)**
5) After Simpson and Madame Lalande got married, Simpson found Madame Lalande was an old woman. **(F)**

3. Multiple choice

1) Madame Lalande accepted Robert's proposal because _____
   A. she was moved by Robert's enthusiasm.
   B. she liked Robert very much.
   C. she wanted to teach Robert a lesson.

2) The night before the wedding, Madame Lalande asked Robert to _____
   A. put on the spectacles.
   B. turn on the light.
   C. tell her age.

3) How did Madame Lalande try to make herself look good?

   A. <u>With the help of powder and wig.</u>

   B. With the help of spectacles.

   C. With the help of her granddaughter.

4) How did Robert feel when he put on the spectacles and looked at Madame Lalande?

   A. He felt satisfied.

   B. He felt proud.

   C. <u>He felt shocked.</u>

5) Robert never again went without the spectacles because _____

   A. <u>he learned a good lesson.</u>

   B. his eyes were worse.

   C. he had married a beautiful woman.

4. Questions for discussion

1) What kind of person is Robert Simpson?

Robert was a vain young man who attached too much importance to his physical appearance. In order to make himself attractive, he refused to wear spectacles although he would suffer much from his decision since he couldn't see well.

Robert was romantic and enthusiastic. His intense feeling at the first sight of Madame Lalande and his marriage proposal to her very soon afterwards revealed that he was ready to devote himself to a romantic love.

Robert was also impatient and rash. He proposed to Madame Lalande before they had time to know each other well.

2) It is said women are more vain(爱虚荣的) than men. Do you believe that?

Some people say that vanity only exists in women. It is not true. Vanity finds its existence in every person's mind, only to different degrees. A proper measure of vanity can be a good stimulus for people to keep self-respect, but too much of it will lead to mistakes, even disasters. Of course, vanity takes different forms for men and women. A man's vanity is always revealed through his expectations about money and position, while a woman's vanity is often shown through her physical appearance. The young man in the text is an exception to this observation since his vanity is in his appearance instead of other things.

V. A tip for performance

（略）

VI. Self-assessment

（略）

VII. Homework

（略）

Mrs. McWilliams and the Lightning

I. Learning something about drama

1. A card about drama

(additional information)

Costume

Costume has always been a major element in the theatrical experience. Modern costume design serves important functions. The costumes of a play show us what sort of world we are asked to enter, not only by its historical place and period but its social and cultural values as well. The individual costumes can express the specific individuality of each character's role. They reveal at a glance, for example, the character's profession, wealth, age, class status, taste, and self-image. More subtly, costume can suggest the character's vices（恶）, virtues（善）, and hidden hopes or fears. By the use of color, shape, fabric, even the sound a fabric makes, costume designers can imbue（赋予）every character with distinct individuality.

Makeup

Makeup is essentially the design of the actor's face. Makeup is the means by which the actor changes his or her appearance to resemble that of the character. For example, makeup helps to make a young actor look older in order to resemble a known historical figure. The modern makeup artist may try to suggest character by exaggerating or distorting the actor's natural eye placement, the size and shape of his or her mouth, the angularity（棱角）of his or her nose, or the tilt（倾斜）of his or her eyebrows. They make impressions of a character's inner state on the basis of observable physical characteristics.

2. Try by yourself

Characters' costume tells the time when the events in the play take place. Please arrange the costumes in the following pictures according to time order (from early to present time).

Picture 1   Picture 3   Picture 2

II. Preparation for learning

1. Questions to think about

Do you have any superstitions? Have you heard of any superstitions practiced by people in the West?

Some of the Western people have superstitions such as:

Many people believe in lucky and unlucky days, numbers, signs and jewels.

Many people regard Friday as an unlucky day — as a bad day to begin a journey, to marry, or to make any investment.

It is thought by many that it is dangerous for thirteen people to dine together.

It is believed that breaking a mirror brings bad luck.

It is said mixed red and white flowers are considered ominous, because in Roman times flowers of those colors were placed on lovers' graves.

It is believed whistling is taboo because it may call up a storm.

When a family moves to a new home it would take embers from the old fireplace and burn them in the new one, to signify that family ties will remain unbroken.

Never put your shoes on the bed, because that means a death in your family.

If a wild bird flies into your house, that is a sign of death.

2. The whole story of the play

At the opening of the story, frightened of the lightening storm that seems to be raging outside, Mrs. McWilliams is hiding in the closet. She protests against her husband's every act because she thinks it is dangerous to make such movements in a thunderstorm. She does not allow her husband Mortimer to open the door, light a match, put on clothes, sing a song or stand by the fireplace, all of which may attract lightning in the eyes of Mrs. McWilliams.

Then, however, she herself lights a match in order to read the directions in a German book, which teaches people how to avoid being struck by lightning. She asks her husband to stand on a chair with heavy fireman's helmet and ring a large dinner bell to avoid being killed by lightning. Their neighbors hear the noise and come to their house to make inquiries, and tell them the sound of thunder they hear and the flashes of lightning they see is produced by the cannon people shoot in order to celebrate the nomination of Garfield as the president.

3. Words and expressions

■ **frightened**
The little boy is frightened of fire.
这个小男孩很怕火。

■ **hit**
A powerful earthquake hit the city.
这个城市遭受了一次强烈的地震。

■ **ashamed**
I am ashamed of myself for being so stupid.
我因我自己这么愚蠢而感到惭愧。

■ **strike**
The village was struck by drought.
这个村子遭受了旱灾。

■ **attract**
The traffic accident attracted a large crowd.
交通事故吸引了一大群人。

■ **interrupt**
A knock at the door interrupted his thoughts.
敲门声打断了他的思路。

■ **flow**
The doctor stopped the flow of blood.
医生把血止住了。

■ **complicated**
The story is too complicated for the children.

这个故事对小孩子来说太复杂了。

- **annoy**

  She was annoyed at his rude attitude.

  她对他粗鲁的态度感到很生气。

- **instant**

  I was going to sleep and at that very instant the telephone rang.

  我刚要入睡，就在那时候电话铃响了。

- **keep up**

  She kept up her spirits very well despite all her bad luck.

  虽然遭受种种厄运，她依然毫不气馁。

- **for one's sake**

  I tell the truth for your sake.

  因为你的缘故我说了真话。

- **put out**

  He put out the cigarette and went to bed.

  他灭了香烟去睡觉。

III. Script

人物

叙述人

莫泰默尔·麦克威廉斯：一个安静的丈夫，竭尽全力让妻子高兴，以保持家庭的安宁

伊万吉琳·麦克威廉斯：一个歇斯底里的妻子

伯莎：一个小女孩，麦克威廉斯夫妇的女儿

叙述人：有些人害怕黑暗。有些人害怕动物。而有些人害怕雷电暴雨，麦克威廉斯夫人就是其中之一。

伊万吉琳：莫泰默尔！莫泰默尔！

莫泰默尔：(睡意蒙眬)呣？怎么了？是谁呀？

伊万吉琳：莫泰默尔！快醒醒！快醒醒！

莫泰默尔：伊万吉琳！你在哪里？我听到了你的声音但是我看不到你。

伊万吉琳：在这里……在衣橱里，还有伯莎。

莫泰默尔：你在衣橱里做什么？现在应该是午夜了吧。

声音：(劈啪的雷响声)

伊万吉琳：(尖叫)你听到了吗？这就是为什么我们要躲在衣橱里。伯莎，你还好吗，亲爱的？

伯莎：是的，妈妈。我还好。

声音：(雷的响声)

伊万吉琳：越来越厉害了。房子要被击中了。我们都会死的。我知道我们会的！伯莎，你还好吗？

伯莎：是的，妈妈。我一分钟以前告诉过你我还好。

伊万吉琳：勇敢的孩子。为了她的妈妈保持了勇气。莫泰默尔，你在做什么？

莫泰默尔：我什么也没做。我正躺在床上。

伊万吉琳：躺在床上？莫泰默尔！这是最危险的地方。

莫泰默尔：危险？

伊万吉琳：所有的书上都这么说！你应该为自己感到羞愧，还睡觉呢。我们随时会被闪电击中的。

莫泰默尔：我很抱歉，伊万吉琳。伯莎，你还好吗，亲爱的？

伯莎：是的，爸爸。但在衣橱里太热了。

莫泰默尔：那我把门打开透些新鲜空气进来。

伊万吉琳：莫泰默尔，别碰那门！

伯莎：但是妈妈，这里实在太热了，我都快不能呼吸了！

伊万吉琳：但那样的话当闪电穿过房顶的时候就伤不着你了。别碰那门，莫泰默尔。

莫泰默尔：好吧，亲爱的。我进衣橱来与你和伯莎呆在一起。

伊万吉琳：没地方了。实际上我们两个人已经够挤了。告诉我，你现在在哪里？还在窗户边上吗？

莫泰默尔：不，伊万吉琳。我没站在窗户边上。我在找我的鞋子。

伊万吉琳：你点火柴了吗？

莫泰默尔：当然点了。黑漆漆的我找不到鞋子。

伊万吉琳：莫泰默尔，你疯了吗？没什么东西能比亮光更能引来闪电了。这是你做的最糟糕的事。马上把它灭了。

声音：(雷的响声)

伊万吉琳：听到了吗？我敢肯定就是那根火柴引来的闪电。

莫泰默尔：我很抱歉，伊万吉琳。

伊万吉琳：你很抱歉！当你的妻子和女儿死在这里的时候你会更抱歉。

伯莎：妈妈！别那样说！你吓着我了。

伊万吉琳：噢，这是真的。你在哪里？莫泰默尔，回到床上了吗？

莫泰默尔：不，伊万吉琳，我正在穿衣服。

声音：(雷的响声)

伊万吉琳：穿衣服？你一点理智也没有了吗？马上把衣服脱掉！你很清楚羊毛会引来闪电。

莫泰默尔：好吧，如果你这样说的话。(开始自己唱起歌来。)

伊万吉琳：你在唱歌吗，莫泰默尔？

莫泰默尔：是的，伊万吉琳。我的嗓子不怎么样，但我还是喜欢试着唱唱。

伊万吉琳：我告诉过你一千遍的是什么？唱歌会引起震动。震动会干扰电的流动……而且……噢，这解释起来太复杂了。你现在在哪里，莫泰默尔？

莫泰默尔：我在火炉旁边。

伊万吉琳：你总是做让我恼火的事情。即使伯莎也知道那是最糟糕的地方。

伯莎：这不对，妈妈。我以前从来没听说过这样的事。

伊万吉琳：不，你听过的。只不过你忘记了。莫泰默尔！现在就离开火炉。火炉是闪电的最佳导体！

莫泰默尔：我能去哪儿？我每动一下你就叫我到别的地方去！

声音：（雷的响声）

IV. Reflections and discussions

1. Write a summary of the script by filling in the blanks with the given words.

> lit   conductor   attract   vibration   bolt   struck

> At the beginning, Mrs. McWilliams was hiding in the clothes closet to avoid being *struck* by lightning. She didn't allow her husband Mortimer to lie on the bed because all the books said it was dangerous; she protested when her husband wanted to open the door because a closed door would keep the *bolt* away; she was angry when her husband *lit* a match because she was sure light would *attract* lightning. She ordered her husband to stop singing because she thought *vibration* would cause lightning. She was annoyed when her husband stood by the fireplace because she believed that the fireplace was the best *conductor* for lightning.

2. True or false

1) Evangeline was afraid of everything, especially lightning. **(F)**
2) Evangeline and her daughter were hiding in the closet because they believed there was a terrible storm. **(T)**
3) Evangeline thought the bed was the most dangerous place. **(T)**
4) Evangeline asked her husband not to lie on the bed and come into the closet. **(F)**
5) Mortimer did not have a good voice but he liked to sing. **(T)**

3. Multiple choice

1) Why did Evangeline say Mortimer should be ashamed of himself when he lied on bed?
   A. Because she thought that it was dangerous for him to do so.
   B. Because he should stay with the family in the closet.
   C. Because he should open the door to let in some fresh air.

2) What did Evangeline forbid Mortimer to do?
   A. Close the door.
   B. Stand by the fireplace.
   C. Find his shoes.

3) Mortimer wanted to open the door because _____

    A. he felt hot in the room.

    B. <u>Bertha felt hard to breathe in the closet.</u>

    C. he wanted to leave the house.

4) Evangeline did not allow Mortimer to put on clothes because she thought _____

    A. it would make him feel hotter.

    B. it would cause vibration.

    C. <u>it would invite lightning.</u>

5) What did Evangeline think about the lightning?

    A. <u>She would be struck by the lightning at any minute.</u>

    B. The lightning was the worst she had ever seen.

    C. The lightning would make her daughter brave.

4. Questions for discussion

1) What do you think of Evangeline's belief about electrical storms?

    In fact, Evangeline had no reason to be so afraid of electric storms. She lost her self-possession in front of a flash of lightning, and her fright was something funny and pitiable to see. Because she had little knowledge about weather and nature, she drove herself into panic and made a fool of herself. Her lack of common senses made her hysterical and helpless, and made a cause for the suffering of the whole family.

2) What should people do in order to get rid of wrong beliefs or superstitions?

    Since the foundation of superstition is ignorance, people should learn scientific knowledge so as to have a clear idea of what nature and life is all about.

    Because people are likely to believe in superstitions especially in times of danger or emergency, they should train themselves to remain calm, try to think about the true relation between cause and effect, and find an effective solution.

    People may have superstitions when they have unusual and unexplainable experience. If they can communicate with their friends about their experience, they may find a proper explanation, reach a correct understanding, and thus get rid of their wrong beliefs and free themselves from unnecessary troubles.

V. A tip for performance

（略）

VI. Self-assessment

（略）

VII. Homework

（略）

Uncle Tom's Cabin

I. Learning something about drama

1. A card about drama

(additional information)

Two notions of acting

Since the first discussions of acting, which date from Greek times, theatre artists have recognized two different notions of acting.

The first notion is that acting is something that the actor "presents" to the audience — through an ability to imitate different characters and their individual and social styles. Such acting is sometimes called "presentational," "external," or "technical": the actor learns to present a role through a program of training — not from inside the actor but from an instructional process that includes formal analysis, technical lessons and drills, and often the imitation of teachers, well-known actors and other students.

The second notion of acting emphasizes the inside of the actor. By studying the role closely and entering the world of the play through her or his own imagination, the actor works to honestly and effectively "live the life of the character" within the play's situation. To do this, the actor must actually "feel" the emotion of the character and even feel that she or he "is"— during the moments of performance — the character. This is generally considered the "internal" or "representational" notion of acting.

2. Try by yourself

Decide whether the following statements are about presentational acting or representational acting.

1) The actor must actually feel the emotions of the character. (representational)
2) In order to move the audience, the actor must first be moved himself. (representational)
3) A great actor must be an unmoved onlooker. (presentational)
4) Actors impress the public not when they are furious, but when they play fury well. (presentational)

II. Preparation for learning

1. Questions to think about

Do you find any inequalities in this world? What are they?

There are still some inequalities existing in this world.

There is racial inequality such as that between black people and white people. In the United States, black children used not to be allowed to enter the same school with the white children. Even today, black people have fewer chances than white people to hold important positions in the government.

There is inequality between men and women. Women are sometimes regarded as inferior to men in every aspect in social life all around the world. Women are often paid less than men for the same work, and few women hold important positions in the government or a company. In some countries or areas, women's place is still considered to be at home.

There is inequality between the rich and the poor. The gap between the rich and the poor leads to their different rights in politics, economy and education. The link between poverty and poor education and low income is obvious to notice.

Just as among the individuals, inequality is also quite common among the countries. The powerful developed countries, such as the United States, set the international standards, which are always used to protect the rich countries but harm the poor countries.

2. The whole story of the play

Uncle Tom's Cabin (1852) is written by American writer Harriet Beecher Stowe. The story opens with two men sitting in a parlor. Haley, a slave trader, was discussing how Mr. Shelby, the plantation owner, could pay off his debts. Shelby was trying to sell his slave, Tom, who had been his loyal servant since boyhood, and five-year-old Harry, who, called Jim Crow by his master Shelby, was a beautiful and talented child. Shelby hesitated about separating the child from his mother, Eliza. Eliza overheard Mrs. Shelby, a very religious woman, protesting about her husband's decision, and decided to flee the plantation with her son. George, her husband, also a slave from a neighboring plantation, had already left for Canada via the "underground railroad," a secret network of people who ushered runaway slaves to freedom in the North. Eliza planned to do the same, and tried to convince Uncle Tom to save himself and come with her. Uncle Tom, however, remained loyal to his master, despite the risk of death at the cruel hands of a new master, and did not go with Eliza. She finally managed to reunite with her husband George, and the whole family arrived in Canada with the help of an anti-slavery organization. Tom was resold to different masters for several times, and at last died at the hand of a merciless drunkard Legree. The novel ended with a chapter summarizing the lesson learned from these "sketches" of experiences with slavery: that slavery is indeed a very cruel and evil institution that should be abolished.

3. Words and expressions

■ **arrange**

He arranged the contacts between the two companies.

他安排两个公司之间的接触。

■ **trade**

He works in the cotton trade.

他做棉花生意。

■ **capable**

He is a capable lawyer.

他是个能干的律师。

■ **square**

His dealings are not always quite square.

他办事有时候路子不太正。

■ **pray**

In church they prayed to God for the sick child.

他们在教堂里为生病的小孩向上帝祈祷。

■ **valuable**

The experience was very valuable.

这一经历非常有价值。

- **spare**

Can you spare ten minutes to discuss the problem?

你能抽出 10 分钟的时间来讨论一下这个问题吗?

- **settle**

The problem was settled to his satisfaction.

这个问题解决得让他很满意。

- **avoid**

You should avoid being late for your class.

你应该避免上课迟到。

- **think over**

Fishing gives people a good chance to think things over.

钓鱼可以给人一个仔细考虑问题的好机会。

- **carry on**

They carried on the discussion late into the night.

他们一直讨论到深夜。

- **in the meantime**

I will call you Sunday, but in the meantime say nothing.

我星期天给你打电话,但在此期间什么也别说。

III. Script

汤姆叔叔的小屋

人物:

谢尔贝先生: 黑奴汤姆的主人

海利: 一个奴隶贩子

场景:

2 月里的某日下午,寒气袭人。在一间陈设精致的客厅里,有两位绅士对坐小酌。

谢尔贝先生: 我看这事就这么办吧。　　**海利:** 这买卖我做不了,谢尔贝先生。(举

起酒杯）

谢尔贝先生：可是，海利，事实是，汤姆不是一般的人，他值这个价。他稳重、诚实、能干，把我的整个庄园管理得井井有条。

海利：你是说黑人那种诚实吧？（倒了一杯白兰地）

谢尔贝先生：不，我是说实话。汤姆的确是个虔诚的好人。四年前，他在一次野外的布道会上皈依了基督教，我相信他是诚心诚意的。从此以后，我就把全部产业——钱、房子、马匹，全都交给他管，并且让他自由行动。汤姆处处表现得忠实可靠。

海利：有些人根本就不相信有虔诚的黑奴，我倒是信。我上次贩到奥尔良的那个黑奴就是这么一个家伙——听到他祷告挺让人舒服，性情很驯和，也很安静。我在他身上赚了一大笔钱，因为当时我买他的价格很便宜。说实话，我认为一个黑奴信教确有好处。

谢尔贝先生：哦，汤姆非常诚实。去年秋天，我打发他去辛辛那提帮我办事，顺便捎带 500 块钱回来。我告诉他我信得过他，因为他是个基督徒，他永远也不会欺骗我。

海利：他回来了吗？

谢尔贝先生：不出所料，他回来了。有人问他为什么不逃到加拿大去。他回答说："噢，主人信任我。我不能这么干。"

海利：看上去他真是件好货。唔，除了汤姆以外，再额外添上个男孩或小姑娘，行不行？

谢尔贝先生：咳！我实在没有多余的人的。不瞒你说，我卖黑奴是万不得已的事。我实在不想和我的人手分开。这是事实。

海利：刚才我在你的花园前看到了一个很可爱的小男孩。（他突然拍了一下谢尔贝先生的肩膀）你把这小男孩卖给我，这笔买卖就这么结了。一言为定。

谢尔贝先生：这孩子是不能卖的。不瞒你说，我这人还比较仁慈，不忍心把这孩子和他母亲拆开。

海利：噢，是吗？哎，我完全能体谅。这种事总叫人不舒服。你看，我做这行买卖，总是避免这样不愉快的场面。你把他母亲弄到别的地方呆上一天或一个礼拜，那么事情就可以被悄悄地解决。眼不见，心不烦嘛。

谢尔贝先生：这事我还得考虑考虑。同时，如果你想按你说的那样人不知、鬼不觉的把事情办得熨熨帖帖的话，那你最好别在邻近一带走漏消息。

海利：噢，那当然！但我告诉你，我的时间紧迫得很，希望能尽快得到你的答复。（站起来穿上外衣）

谢尔贝先生：好，那么你今晚6点到7点之间来听回音吧。（他陪同海利一起走到门口）

IV. Reflections and discussions

1. Write a summary of the script by filling in the blanks with the given words.

settle	spare	throw	deal	capable	parlor

The story opened with two men sitting in a *parlor*. Haley, a slave trader, was discussing how Mr. Shelby, the plantation owner, could pay off his debts. Shelby was trying to sell his slave, Tom, who was honest and *capable*, but Haley did not think that Tom was enough for the debt and asks for another slave to <u>settle</u> the business. Shelby said that he had none to *spare*. Haley wanted Shelby to *throw* a little black boy into the *deal* with Tom. Shelby said that he did not like to break up families, but Haley said that if they got the black mother off for a few days, the thing would be done quietly. Shelby told him he would think about it and tell Haley his answer later that evening.

2. True or false

1) Haley thought that Tom was worth the price his owner demanded. **(F)**

2) Mr. Shelby thought Tom was honest and capable. **(T)**

3) Haley did not believe there was any pious Negro. **(F)**

4) Mr. Shelby hated to take the boy away from his mother. **(T)**

5) Mr. Shelby asked Haley to keep secret about their trade. **(T)**

3. Multiple choice

1) Mr. Shelby believed Tom was a good slave because Tom was _____

    A. <u>capable and honest.</u>

    B. clever and quiet.

    C. gentle and quiet.

2) Mr. Shelby trusted Tom because _____

    A. he loved Tom very much.

    B. <u>Tom was a Christian.</u>

    C. Tom was capable.

3) Which statement is true about Tom?

    A. He believed religion in his childhood.

    B. He never left the farm.

    C. <u>He was good at managing the farm.</u>

4) Why did Haley advise Mr. Shelby to send the mother away for some days?

    A. Because he thought it would reduce the pain of the mother.

    B. Because he thought it would do good to the child.

C. Because he thought it would save him much trouble.

5) Why did Mr. Shelby not want to sell the little boy?

A. Because Mr. Shelby didn't want to separate him from his mother.

B. Because Mr. Shelby was not in need of money.

C. Because Mr. Shelby trusted the little boy.

4. Questions for discussion

1) How do you understand the personal characteristics of Haley and Shelby?

Haley was a cruel person. He had no regard for the family love that the "niggers" might have. He even advised Mr. Shelby to take the mother away when he came to collect the little boy so that they would be spared unnecessary tears. Though he claimed to believe in religion, it was clear that money was always more important than his conscience.

To some degree, Mr. Shelby treated his slaves with kindness and consideration. Nevertheless, he still considered them his disposable property in time of need. He recognized Tom's good qualities, and highlighted them when he was negotiating his sale.

2) What should people do to eliminate racial discrimination?

There are many things people should do to eliminate racial discrimination.

First, black people should strive to be more independent economically and politically. Only when independence is achieved can black people be treated equally.

Secondly, black people should strengthen their tie and have more cooperation with each other. Unity brings power.

Thirdly, international organizations should be established and international laws should be made to regulate the relationship between the black and the white, to prevent the abuse of power by the white, and to protect the rights of the black.

Fourthly, educational programs or TV programs should be made to raise people's awareness of racism, and make people understand that all men are equal. Racism is a kind of moral corruption and a violation of human rights.

V. A tip for performance

（略）

VI. Self-assessment

（略）

VII. Homework

（略）

Washington Square

I. Learning something about drama

1. A card about drama

(additional information)

Broadway, off-Broadway and off-off-Broadway

Broadway is the longest street in Manhattan. The world knows it mainly for its cluster of thirty-some theatres in the dozen blocks north of Times Square. Broadway's charm is its visual and social excitement, its bright lights and famed celebrities, and its trend-setting fashions, big-buck（钱）entertainment, and high-toned（时尚的，不凡的）Tony Awards. The stakes are higher on Broadway than anywhere else in theatre; if you can make it here, you'll make it anywhere.

Broadway is no longer the place where new plays originate. Rather it has become, primarily, the staging ground for extravagantly（豪华地）produced musicals. Also, it is the showcase for the best (or at least most commercially promising) new plays from America's regional theatres. Rarely does a new play by a young playwright premiere（首次公演）on Broadway. The costs are far too high to risk on an unknown author. Finally, it is the site of major revivals of classic dramas that form the American and international repertory.

Not all of New York drama is performed within the Broadway district. There are hundreds of theatres called "off-Broadway" theatres. Off-Broadway, a term that came into existence during the 1950s, refers to professional theatres operating on significantly reduced budget. They are found primarily in Greenwich Village, with some in the area south of Houston Street and other on the upper East and West Sides of Manhattan. Yet another category of theatre is known as off-off-Broadway, a term dating from the 1960s that refers to semiprofessional or even amateur theatres located in the metropolitan area, often in church basements, YMCAs, coffeehouses, and converted studios or garages.

Much of the original creative work in the American theatre since World War II has been done in the off-Broadway and off-off-Broadway theatres, and their generally original works have attracted large audience to see original works before they are showcased to the Broadway masses.

2. Try by yourself

Picture 1 *Les Miserables*（《悲惨世界》）

Picture 2 *The Cats*（《猫》）

Picture 3 *The Phantom of the Opera*（《剧院魅影》）

Picture 4 *Miss Saigon*（《西贡小姐》）

II. Preparation for learning

1. Questions to think about

Do you think old people and young people always hold different opinions? Why?

More often than not old people and young people hold different opinions. Young people like to act on the spot without much thinking. It is regarded as one of the ways for the youth to show that they have grown up and they can independently and effectively face any difficult situation. The young are always more intuitive and impulsive in their decisions and actions. But older people have learned too much lessons from their life experience to be rash, and they always tend to take more into consideration before they make an important decision. The senior people are more patient and cautious.

Young people long for independence and they do not want the old people to say "yes" or "no" to what they do. All they want is to do what they consider proper, after so many years of childhood under the control of the grown-ups. But they haven't always won the old people's trust, and it is very common for the old people to interfere with what they do. Thus, there is something we call "generation gap."

2. The whole story of the play

Washington Square (1880) is written by famous American novelist Henry James. This story takes place in the Manhattan neighborhood of Washington Square in the mid-nineteenth century. Dr. Austin Sloper is a respectable physician. His wife gives birth to a daughter named Catherine and dies in childbirth. Dr. Sloper is disappointed in Catherine. She is not a boy; she is neither so pretty as her mother, nor so intelligent as her father. At a party Catherine meets Morris Townsend, an eloquent and very good-looking young man. The doctor sees through Morris: a lazy person who regards Catherine as the source of his fortune. At the same time, Aunt Lavinia, a younger sister of Dr. Sloper, does everything to encourage the romance between Morris and Catherine. Though Morris's primary motivation is economic, he is kind to Catherine and treats her with far more affection and consideration than Dr. Sloper does. Consequently, Dr. Sloper finds it difficult to make Catherine leave Morris, so he vows if Catherine marries Morris, he will disown her as his daughter. He also asks her to accompany him on a trip to Europe, hoping that the separation will split the two, but Catherine remains firm in her intent. Realizing that Catherine will lose her inheritance from her father, Morris backs out of the courting. Catherine's heart is broken. When Dr. Sloper is near death, he asks Catherine to promise that she won't marry Morris. But Catherine is so offended by the doctor's rude attitude that she stubbornly refuses to make any vow. In the end, before he dies, Dr. Sloper gives most of his fortune to charity. A few years after Sloper's death, Morris Townsend returns, having learned that Catherine has never married. When he meets Catherine again, Catherine is upset and dismisses Townsend after a few minutes of conversation. Catherine continues to live unmarried, devoting herself to and finding value and pleasure in hobbies and interests.

3. Words and expressions

■ **inherit**

A son inherits his father.

子承父业。

■ **impress**

I was impressed by his talent.

他的才干给我留下了深刻的印象。

■ **apply**

He applied for the job last week.

他上个星期申请了那份工作。

■ **position**

This position can best be filled by a college-trained man.

这一职位最好由受过大学教育的男子担任。

■ **address**

He addressed his thanks to the host.

他对主人表示感谢。

■ **honor**

I have the honor to present the governor.

我很荣幸地向大家介绍总督。

■ **involve**

The investigation involved many innocent people.

这次调查牵涉到很多无辜的人。

■ **consideration**

Cost is a major consideration in buying anything.

买东西时价钱是主要的考虑因素。

■ **estate**

He is a man of small estate.

他的家产不多。

■ **deny**

He denies I ever told him.

他否认我曾经告诉过他。

■ **offer**

He made an offer of assistance.

他主动提出给予帮助。

■ **nothing but**

She could see nothing but his head.

除了他的头以外，她什么也看不见。

■ **be aware of**

I was not aware of the danger.

我没有意识到危险。

■ **in exchange for**

He gave me an apple in exchange for a piece of cake.

他给了我一个苹果以交换一块蛋糕。

III. Script

华盛顿广场

人物:

叙述人

凯瑟琳·斯洛普

莫里斯·汤森

拉维妮亚·潘尼曼夫人: 凯瑟琳的阿姨

奥斯丁·斯洛普医生: 凯瑟琳的父亲

叙述人: 在纽约华盛顿广场的一幢漂亮的老房子里,住着奥斯丁·斯洛普医生和他的女儿凯瑟琳。斯洛普医生很有钱,他的女儿有朝一日会继承一大笔遗产。斯洛普医生的妹妹拉维妮亚和他们住在一起。她很为凯瑟琳的婚事着急。有一天,凯瑟琳在一次聚会上认识了一个年轻人。他的名字叫莫里斯·汤森。从那次聚会后,莫里斯每天都来找凯瑟琳。潘尼曼夫人对他印象很好,并极力撮合他们的恋情。有一天她对她哥哥谈到了莫里斯。

拉维妮亚: 我敢肯定你会喜欢他,奥斯丁。他是一个非常讨人喜欢的年轻人。而且很英俊。难道他不是你见过最漂亮的男人吗,凯瑟琳?

凯瑟琳: 噢,他很优雅。

斯洛普医生: 英俊?优雅?那他的家庭呢?他靠什么谋生?

拉维妮亚: 我们不能问那样的问题。毕竟他不是在求职。

斯洛普医生: 谁知道呢?也许他就想那样。也许他听说了凯瑟琳将要继承的遗产。他可能想找的工作就是当她的丈夫。

凯瑟琳: 父亲,那样说是不公平的!

斯洛普医生: 我并不是在对他下判断。我只是在问一些必须要问的问题。我是个实际的人,拉维妮亚。我相信汤森的目的是她的钱。他还能看上别的什么呢?凯瑟琳不漂亮。她也不聪明。她除了钱以外一无所有。我不想把我的钱留给一个追逐钱财的人。

拉维妮亚: 奥斯丁,你心里一点浪漫情趣也没有。

斯洛普医生: 哦,我亲爱的妹妹,你心里的浪漫情趣太多了。

拉维妮亚: 门铃响了。莫里斯来了。我去开门让他进来。

凯瑟琳: 父亲,请对汤森先生好一点。

斯洛普医生: 你这话是什么意思,凯瑟琳?我对每个人都总是很好。

莫里斯: 下午好,斯洛普小姐。很高兴再次见到你。

凯瑟琳：下午好，汤森先生。

莫里斯：能与著名的斯洛普医生相会我感到非常愉快。很高兴见到您，先生。我长久以来一直期待着这份荣幸。

斯洛普医生：谢谢你，汤森先生。我很高兴见到你。请坐。

莫里斯：谢谢你，先生。

斯洛普医生：你今天能来喝茶真是很好，汤森先生。我想像你是个很忙的人。没有多少年轻人愿意挤出他们的工作时间。

莫里斯：您可以这么理解，我现在正在度假什么的，斯洛普医生。

斯洛普医生：我明白。我相信你来这里的目的是关于我女儿的。

莫里斯：是的，斯洛普医生。我想娶凯瑟琳。我们已经彼此相爱了。

斯洛普医生：我明白。看到年轻人相爱总是件好事。但是，一旦涉及到婚姻，就有许多要考虑的问题。当然你已经意识到了她的财富。她从她母亲那里继承了地产，我死之后她还会继承更多。当然，除非我决定改变我的遗嘱。

莫里斯：我对她的钱一无所知。我只知道我爱她。我想和她结婚。

斯洛普医生：我很高兴听到你这么说。但是，我们不能否认她的钱是个很重要的考虑因素。因此，我想问你几个问题。

莫里斯：我很乐意回答。

斯洛普医生：好的。首先，你靠什么谋生？

莫里斯：我能从自己拥有的一些财产上获得一点收入。

斯洛普医生：但你有工作吗？

莫里斯：是的，我有。我给我姐姐的孩子当家教，换取我在她家里的食宿费用。

斯洛普医生：就这些？

莫里斯：目前为止是这样。但我有几份非常好的工作机会。我正在对其中的一两个进行考虑。

斯洛普医生：你还没有决定？

莫里斯：是的，还没有决定。

斯洛普医生：那么恐怕我不能给你任何答复了。坦率地说，汤森先生，我并没有把你当作我的女婿。

莫里斯：你为什么不考虑一下你女儿的感受？

斯洛普医生：我当然会考虑。但除非事情发生了转变，事情只能如此。

IV. Reflections and discussions

1. Write a summary of the script by filling in the blanks with the given words.

impressed   son-in-law   interviewed   elegant   inheritance   intend

Lavinia was *impressed* by Morris and thought he was handsome and *elegant*. But Dr. Sloper thought he pursued Catherine for the sake of her *inheritance*, and he didn't *intend* to leave his money to a fortune hunter. Then Dr. Sloper *interviewed* Morris about his background, and was not satisfied with his answers because he had only a little income and had not a steady job. At last Dr. Sloper told Morris he did not see him as his *son-in-law*.

2. True or false

1) Catherine was a beautiful and rich girl. **(F)**

2) Lavinia wanted Catherine to marry Morris. **(T)**

3) Dr. Sloper believed that Morris was a fortune hunter. **(T)**

4) Catherine is likely to have an inheritance not only from her father but also from her mother.

   (T)

5) Morris tutored his sister's children in order to get room and board. **(T)**

3. Multiple choice

1) Why was Lavinia impressed by Morris?

   A. Because he was rich and handsome.

   B. <u>Because he was pleasant and good-looking.</u>

   C. Because he was rich and elegant.

2) What did Dr. Sloper think of Catherine?

   A. He thought Catherine was clever.

   B. He thought Catherine had nothing.

   C. <u>He thought Catherine was plain.</u>

3) What did Dr. Sloper think of Morris?

   A. He thought Morris was applying for a job in his firm.

   B. <u>He thought Morris was after Catherine's inheritance.</u>

   C. He thought Morris was not aware of Catherine's wealth.

4) Which statement is true about Morris?

   A. <u>Morris tutored his sister's children in order to get room and board.</u>

   B. Morris had several excellent offers but he refused to consider them.

   C. Morris had neither income nor work.

5) Why did Dr. Sloper ask Morris those questions?

   A. Because he wanted to know if Morris was willing to answer his questions.

   B. <u>Because he wanted to know if Morris was after Catherine's inheritance.</u>

   C. Because he wanted to know if Morris wanted to marry Catherine.

4. Questions for discussion

1) Do you think Morris was after Catherine's money?

Most probably Morris was after Catherine's money. From the interview we can find that he had neither sufficient money nor a decent job. The fact that he tutored his sister's children in exchange for his room and board shows that he was in bad need of money and that he was most likely a good-for-nothing. Though he claimed that he had some job offers, judging from his hesitation and uncertainty in the tone of his talking, he was either incapable of doing anything well or unwilling to earn his own living. He was very likely to have lied when he said he didn't know Catherine's inheritance. Morris was a lazy, incompetent, and maybe dishonest fellow. It can be quite safe to say that the doctor was right in his judgment about him.

2) When your parents and you have different opinions about something important to you, what will you do?

When we have different opinions from those of our parents concerning something important to us, we should never lose patience and respect. First, listen to them and think about their opinions carefully. We may insist on what we firmly think is right, but it is quite necessary for us to take in some of their suggestions if our second thoughts tell us they are right. If we cannot accept any of their opinions for the time being, we'd better keep silent, because being angry or excited would not help the situation anyway, but could worsen our relationship with our parents. In addition, there is always middle way that can reconcile the two parties and satisfy both parents and us.

V. A tip for performance

(略)

VI. Self-assessment

(略)

VII. Homework

(略)

The Cop and the Anthem

I. Learning something about drama

1. A card about drama

(additional information)

Tony Award

The formal name of this award is Antoinette Perry Award for Excellence in Theatre. It is presented each June by the American Theatre Wing and the League of American Theatres and Producers to honor distinguished achievement in Broadway Theatre. The first Tony Awards were established in 1947. The major categories of the Tony Awards include: Best Play, Best Musical, Best Performance by a Leading Actress in a Play, Best Performance by a Leading Actor in a Musical and so on.

Pulitzer Prize

The prize was established by Joseph Pulitzer, a Hungarian-American journalist and newspaper publisher in the late 19th century. The first Pulitzer Prizes were awarded in 1917.

New York Drama Critics' Circle Awards

The New York Drama Critics' Circle Awards are presented each May by critics from all New York City's newspapers, magazines and radios except the *New York Times*.

Laurence Olivier Awards

The Laurence Olivier Awards are presented annually by The Society of London Theatre. Nominations are generally announced on the 2nd or 3rd Thursday in January with the winners announced on the 3rd or 4th Friday in February.

London Evening Standard Theatre Awards

The London Evening Standard Theatre Awards are presented annually by the *London Evening Standard Newspaper*. They are normally announced on the last Monday in November. In 2001, for the first time, a short list of nominations were announced on the Tuesday three weeks prior to the Awards presentation. The Awards are normally presented at a special lunch at the Savoy Theatre (by special invite only).

Critics' Circle Awards

The Critics' Circle Awards are presented by the theatre critics from the national and London newspapers and magazines. They are generally announced in early February. The presentation (which is by invite only) has taken place in a variety of venues（地点）around the West End, including a boat on the Thames!

2. Try by yourself

Putting a play production together is an art in itself. There is no normal order in which a play's text, space, people and materials are brought together. In what we call the twentieth-century European model, a director might simply choose a play and begin rehearsing it with a company of actors, designers and technicians, all of whom would work at the same time and cooperate towards the final production.

Please match the pictures with the different steps to put a play production together.

1   Planning meeting of the directors and the designers and staff

2   scene shop

3   costume shop

4   rehearsing

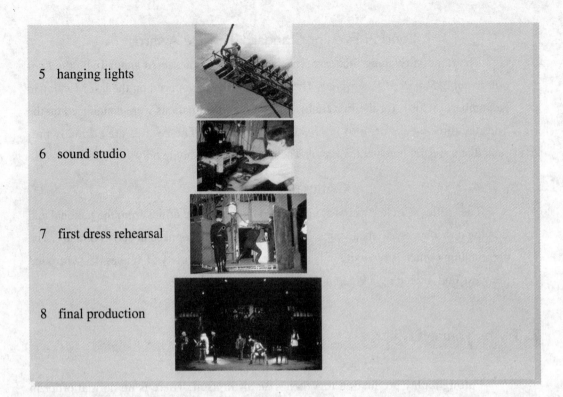

5   hanging lights

6   sound studio

7   first dress rehearsal

8   final production

II. Preparation for learning

1. Question to think about

Under what circumstances is a person likely to make up his mind to change his wrong behavior?

There are many circumstances under which a person may determine to change his behavior.

When a person gets advice from his parents, teachers or friends, and realizes that such advice will do him good in the future, he may decide to turn a new leaf in his life.

When a person reads a book, sees a movie, watches a play or listens to music, he may be moved by the noble characters or the great theme of the artistic works, and may find a motivation to begin a new life.

When a person has some big change, especially the change to a worse situation, in his life, he may feel an urgent need to change his old way because the new change requires him to do so. After all, necessity is always the mother of a purposeful change.

2. The whole story of the play

The Cop and the Anthem is written by famous American writer O. Henry. It takes place in New York, in the late 1800s or early 1900s. Soapy originally lives on a bench in

Madison Square. It is autumn and the leaves are falling. Soapy realizes that winter is coming and he needs to plan something. He can't stay on the park bench because it will snow all winter. Soapy then figures out that he wants to go to "The Island," sa nickname he uses to call a prison in New York. He decides to break the law to get arrested, so he can be fed and warm in the prison for the whole cold winter.

He tries many times to achieve his goal to be imprisoned. He goes, for the first time, to a luxurious restaurant. However, as he is in a miserable dress with a pair of torn shoes, he is kicked off quickly from the place. For a second time, he goes to a for-anyone restaurant. He is welcome there and he orders as many dishes as possible to eat. When the waiter comes to give him the bill, Soapy shows him that he has no money with him and thus he is beaten and then thrown out. He tries to lure a woman, but she turns out to be a prostitute. Also, Soapy tries to pretend to be drunk on the sidewalk. But when the police officers come, they say that they have orders to let these kinds of guys be, because they are celebrating their success in the game, and they are no harm to the public. He tries to steal a man's umbrella, but when he does it, the man gets scared and lets him take it because the man just steals it earlier that day. Finally he becomes totally disappointed and annoyed at his unsuccessful attempts. At last, while walking around a church he hears an anthem being sung. He unconsciously goes near and stays for a while to listen more carefully to that melody. In the meanwhile, Soapy decides to change for the better and live a normal life. Suddenly, a cop comes to him and arrests him for loitering. The next day, the judge sentences him to three months' imprisonment.

3. Words and expressions

■ **attempt**
We succeeded at the first attempt.
我们第一次尝试就成功了。

■ **arrest**
He was arrested ten hours after the murder.
他在谋杀发生10小时后就被逮捕了。

■ **desperate**
The family was in a desperate situation.
那个家庭处于绝境之中。

■ **practice**
He practices playing the piano every day.

他每天练习弹钢琴。

■ **ambition**
He was filled with ambition to become famous.
他一心想成名。

■ **case**
The police studied the murder case.
警方研究了这起谋杀案。

■ **make arrangements for**
I will make arrangements for a car to meet you at the airport.
我将安排一辆汽车来机场接你。

III. Script

警察与赞美诗

人物：
叙述人
警察
索比
法官

叙述人：去年秋天，当天气已经变得很冷，索比无法在晚上睡在公园里的长凳上的时候，他觉得应该为自己过冬做一些打算了。他的计划很简单——去干些违法的事。他确信如果自己犯了法，就会被送进监狱，在冬天的夜晚呆在那里会很暖和。然而，他的几次被捕计划都以失败告终。夜晚降临了，索比感到很绝望。他觉得无论他怎么尝试，今年他都没法进监狱过冬了。他在街上闲荡，来到了一个教堂前面。里面传来了音乐声。是唱诗班正在为下个周日排练歌曲。

索比：多么美的歌声啊。它让我忘记了我所有的问题。这首赞美诗的名字叫什么？小时候我们经常在教堂里唱它。它给我带回了美好的回忆。我那时候的生活是多么不同啊。我是哪里出问题了？我做了什么，让自己堕落得这么厉害？我曾经也有远大的抱负，但看看我现在的样子！我唯一的愿望变成了进监狱。噢，我必须要改变。我还不老。我还有时间开始新的生活。就在上个星期我还得到了一个当卡车司机的工作机会。我敢肯定，只要我想干，我就还能得到那份工作。我明天一早就去看看。在这个世界上我会有一席之地的，我会……

警察（用手抓住索比的手臂）：嘿你！

索比（迅速转过头）：我吗？

警察：对，就是你！你在这个教堂外面做什么？

索比：没做什么。只是听听唱诗班练习唱赞美诗。

警察：听赞美诗？

索比：我路过这个教堂时听到了这首歌，我还是孩子时，我们经常唱它。我就停下来听了。仅此而已。

警察：噢，是吗。那你最好跟我走一趟。法官会对你编的话很感兴趣。

索比：听音乐不算犯罪，不是吗？

警察：不，一点也不算。如果仅此而已，那就罢了。但最近这个居民区发生了一些严重的犯罪事件。说吧！难道今天早些时候我没见过你吗？当然见过了！你就是那个站在第五大街被打碎的窗户前面的那个人！我想无论如何肯定是你把它砸碎的。跟我走吧。

索比：但是警官！

警察：把你的解释省着给法官听吧。走。

叙述人：索比，满腹疑惑地走在警察的后面，被带到了夜间法庭上。

法官：好的。下一个案子。

警察：大人，我在一小时以前发现这个人站在教堂外面。他说他是在听唱诗班唱歌。但还不仅止于此。今天早上我发现站在第五大街被打碎的窗户前面的，也是这个人。

法官：被告还有什么要为自己说的吗？

索比：噢，大人。这位警官说的都是真的。但是……

法官：如果警官说的都是真的，你确实砸碎了窗户，这就没什么好说的了。准备在监狱里待3个月吧。

IV. Reflections and discussions

1. Write a summary of the script by filling in the blanks with the given words.

attempts	failed	desperate	reminded	ambition	crimes

Soapy made several _attempts_ to get arrested, but all of them _failed_. He was _desperate_. When he walked by a church, the anthem from inside brought back the wonderful memories of his childhood and _reminded_ him of the great promise he once had. He regretted that his only _ambition_ was to get into jail and decided to begin a new life. However, a cop came to him and arrested him because he thought Soapy was the person who committed some _crimes_ in the neighborhood lately. At last, the judge sentenced him to 3 months in jail.

2. True or false

1) Soapy wanted to be put into jail because he needed a warm place to live in the winter. **(T)**

2) Soapy was sure that he could get into jail. **(F)**

3) Soapy didn't have a happy childhood. **(F)**

4) Soapy decided to begin a new life because he thought he still had time. **(T)**

5) The judge listened carefully to Soapy's explanation. **(F)**

3. Multiple choice

1) Soapy was desperate when the night had fallen because _____

    A. he hadn't made his plan for the winter.

    B. <u>he couldn't find a warm place for the winter.</u>

    C. he was afraid of being put into jail in the winter.

2) What did Soapy think of when he heard the anthem?

    A. He thought of his miserable childhood.

    B. He thought of his old age.

    C. <u>He thought of his job offer.</u>

3) Having heard the anthem, Soapy decided to _____

    A. get into jail.

    B. <u>apply for the job as a truck driver.</u>

    C. forget all his problems.

4) The policeman asked Soapy to go with him because _____

    A. he believed Soapy's explanation and wanted the judge to hear it.

    B. he believed all the serious crimes in the neighborhood lately were committed by Soapy.

    C. <u>he believed that Soapy broke the window that day.</u>

5) The judge ordered Soapy to spend 3 months in jail because _____

    A. <u>Soapy broke the law.</u>

    B. Soapy lied.

    C. Soapy did not obey the policeman's order.

4. Questions for discussion

1) What kind of person was Soapy?

Soapy was a homeless person and not a bad guy by nature. Although he did something wrong, he didn't want to cause real harm to others. As his single purpose was to find a place to survive the harsh winter, he was different from those ruthless law-breaking criminals. Soapy was also a pitiable person since the prison that is horrific to most people became his best choice to spend the winter.

When the anthem in the church reminded him of his happy childhood and his past ambition, he felt a sudden and magnificent change in his soul. He regretted his sinking and decided to pull himself out of the mire and make a man of himself again. Although Soapy lived as a tramp for many years, he had not totally lost his courage to pursue a new life. He could still feel and hear the call of a decent and meaningful life.

2) Do you think music, or other forms of art, can bring a change in a person's soul and behavior?

Most people believe that music, like any other forms of art, has a function to purify a person's mind and lift his spirits. Because music is a kind of expression of people's feelings and thoughts, when a person is listening to music, he may feel the emotions and spirit expressed in it, recall something which is deeply buried in his memory, develop his imagination triggered off by it, and acquire some new understanding about life and himself. When his feelings and thoughts are actively and fully evoked and motivated by music or other arts, he is most likely to make some important changes that he will never make otherwise.

V. A tip for performance

（略）

VI. Self-assessment

（略）

VII. Homework

（略）

Vocabulary

A

*absolutely *ad.* 绝对地 (U3)

absorbing *a.* 吸引人的 (U1)

address *v.* 对……说话 (U7)

adieu *int.* 再见 (U3)

*advantage *n.* 优势 (U1)

*affair *n.* （恋爱）事件 (U1)

*afterwards *ad.* 后来 (U1)

*ambition *n.* 抱负，野心 (U8)

angel *n.* 天使 (U3)

*annoy *v.* 使恼怒 (U5)

anthem *n.* 赞美诗 (U8)

*anxious *a.* 着急的 (U7)

*apply *v.* 申请 (U7)

*arrange *v.* 安排 (U6)

*arrangement *n.* 安排 (U8)

*arrest *v.* 逮捕 (U8)

article *n.* （物品的）一件 (U6)

as to 关于 (U1)

ashamed *a.* 惭愧的，羞愧的 (U5)

assure *v.* 保证 (U1)

*attempt *n.* 尝试 (U8)

*attract *v.* 吸引 (U5)

*avenue *n.* 大街 (U8)

*avoid *v.* 避免 (U6)

*aware *a.* 意识到的 (U7)

B

battlement *n.* 城垛，高台 (U3)

be aware of 意识到 (U7)

*behave *v.* 举止 (U3)

*behavior *n.* 行为 (U1)

bet *n.* 赌注 (U1)

bolt *n.* 闪电 (U5)

*bored *a.* 无聊的，乏味的 (U1)

*bother *v.* 麻烦 (U1)

*bride *n.* 新娘 (U2)

*brief *a.* 简要的 (U3)

bring back (memory) 带回（记忆） (U8)

C

capable *a.* 能干的 (U6)

carry on 继续，进行 (U6)

*case *n.* 案件 (U8)

*cause *v.* 造成 (U2)

*cheat *v.* 欺骗 (U6)

*choir *n.* 唱诗班 (U8)

Christian *n.* 基督徒 (U6)

*church *n.* 教堂 (U8)

Cincinnati *n.* (地名) 辛辛那提 (U6)

clap *v.* 拍 (U6)

classical *a.* 古典的 (U1)

*class *n.* 阶级 (U1)

closet *n.* 橱柜 (U5)

coax *v.* 哄，劝诱 (U1)

companion *n.* 同伴 (U2)

complicated *a.* 复杂的 (U5)

*concert *n.* 音乐会 (U1)

*conductor *n.* 导体 (U5)

*confused *a.* 困惑的 (U4)

*consideration *n.* 考虑的事物或因素 (U7)

cop *n.* 警察 (U8)

couch *n.* 睡椅 (U3)

court *v.* 求爱 (U4)

*court *n.* 法庭 (U8)

*creature *n.* 人 (U6)

*crime *n.* 罪行 (U3)

crown *n.* 王冠，王权 (U3)

*cruel *a.* 残忍的 (U3)

D

*dawn *n.* 黎明 (U3)

*delighted *a.* 高兴的 (U1)

Denmark *n.* 丹麦 (U3)

deny *v.* 否认 (U7)

devil *n.* 恶魔 (U6)

*desperate *a.* 绝望的 (U8)

dialect *n.* 方言 (U1)

*doubt *v.* 怀疑 (U2)

*dress *v.* 为……穿衣，打扮 (U1)

duchess *n.* 公爵夫人 (U1)

E

earn one's living 谋生 (U1)

earnestly *ad.* 热切地 (U1)

earthly *a.* 尘世的 (U2)

*electrical *a.* 电的 (U5)

*electricity *n.* 电 (U5)

*elegant *a.* 优雅的 (U7)

enormously *ad.* 非常地，极大地 (U1)

*entirely *ad.* 完全地 (U2)

*equal *a.* 平等的

      n. 平等的人或事物 (U2)

*escape *v.* 逃跑 (U6)

estate *n.* 地产，产业 (U7)

*exchange *n.* 交换 (U7)

*explanation *n.* 解释 (U8)

F

fill up 填满 (U1)

fireplace *n.* 火炉 (U5)

*flow *n.* 流动 (U5)

for one's sake 为了某人的缘故 (U5)

*fortune *n.* 财产 (U2)

*frightened *a.* 害怕的 (U5)

G

*generally *ad.* 通常地 (U6)

genius *n.* 天才 (U1)

*gesture *v.* 做手势 (U3)

get over （从震惊、失望、疾病中）恢复 (U4)

ghost *n.* 鬼魂 (U3)

*gift *v.* 赋予 (U2)

governess *n.* 家庭女教师 (U2)

grave *n.* 坟墓 (U2)

gulf *n.* 鸿沟 (U1)

H

*happiness *n.* 幸福 (U2)

heartless *a.* 无情的 (U2)

*hit *v.* 袭击，使遭受 (U5)

*honor *n.* 荣幸 (U7)

*howl *v.* 嚎叫 (U3)

humane *a.* 仁爱的 (U6)

hysterical *a.* 歇斯底里的 (U5)

I

impatient *a.* 不耐烦的 (U1)

*impossible *a.* 不可能的 (U8)

*impress *v.* 使留下深刻印象 (U7)

in exchange for 作为交换 (U7)

in the meantime 在此期间，与此同时 (U6)

incest *n.* 乱伦 (U3)

inherit *v.* 继承 (U7)

inheritance *n.* 遗产 (U7)

*insist *v.* 坚持 (U4)

*instant *n.* （某一）时刻 (U5)

*instead *ad.* 作为替代 (U4)

*intend *v.* 打算 (U2)

*interrupt *v.* 打断 (U5)

*invent *v.* 发明 (U1)

involve *v.* 牵涉 (U7)

Ireland *n.* 爱尔兰 (U2)

J

jail *n.* 监狱 (U8)

*judge *n.* 法官 (U8)

*judge *v.* 判断 (U7)

K

keep up 保持，继续 (U5)

L

lately *ad.* 最近	(U8)	*liquid *n.* 液体	(U3)
liar *n.* 撒谎者	(U2)	*live *a.* 活的，有生命的	(U1)
*light *v.* 点亮	(U5)	lord *n.* 主人，君主	(U3)
*lightning *n.* 闪电	(U5)	lose one's mind 失去理智	(U5)
linguist *n.* 语言学家	(U1)		

M

make arrangements for 为……做好安排	(U8)	*manners *n.* 礼仪	(U1)
make for 朝……走去	(U1)	*master *n.* 主人	(U6)
make one's choice 做出选择	(U2)	momentarily *ad.* 暂时地	(U2)
make one's living 谋生	(U7)	mysterious *a.* 神秘的	(U4)

N

necessity *n.* 必要(性)	(U6)	*noble *a.* 尊贵的	(U3)
*neighborhood *n.* 附近	(U6)	nothing but 除了……以外什么都没有	(U7)
nigger *n.* 黑人，(蔑称) 黑鬼	(U6)		

O

oath *n.* 誓言	(U2)	*order *n.* 常规；秩序	(U1)
obscure *a.* 身份低贱的	(U2)	Orleans *n.* (地名) 奥尔良	(U6)
*offer *v.* 主动提供	(U2)	over-excited *a.* 过分激动的	(U2)
*offer *n.* 给予 (物)，提供 (物)	(U7)		

P

*painful *a.* 痛苦的	(U3)	phonetics *n.* 语音学	(U1)
*paint *n.* 化妆品	(U4)	pick up （无意)得到	(U1)
parlor *n.* 客厅	(U6)	pious *a.* 虔诚的	(U6)
pass off 把……冒充成	(U1)	*plain *a.* 相貌平常的	(U2)
*perfectly *ad.* 完全地	(U6)	*poisonous *a.* 有毒的	(U3)

*position *n.* 职位	(U7)	*promise *n.* 前途，出息	(U8)
*powder *n.* 化妆用粉	(U4)	*properly *ad.* 恰当地	(U1)
*practical *a.* 实际的	(U7)	property *n.* 财产	(U7)
*practice *v.* 练习	(U8)	proposal *n.* 求婚	(U4)
*pray *v.* 祈祷	(U6)	put on 装出……的模样	(U4)
*promise *v.* 保证	(U3)	put out 熄灭，关掉	(U5)

R

revenge *v.* 报仇	(U3)	romance *n.* 浪漫故事	(U7)
*realize *v.* 认识到	(U1)	rouge *n.* 胭脂	(U4)
*refuse *v.* 拒绝	(U3)	*royal *a.* 皇家的，宫廷的	(U3)
*request *n.* 请求	(U4)	rumor *n.* 谣言	(U2)
reveal *v.* 泄漏，揭示	(U3)	run into 偶然遇到	(U2)

S

sealed *a.* 封闭的	(U3)	*soul *n.* 灵魂	(U1)
seduce *v.* 引诱	(U3)	soulless *a.* 没有灵魂的	(U2)
*self *n.* 自我	(U2)	*spare *v.* 抽出	(U6)
*separate *v.* 分开	(U1)	spectacles *n.* 眼镜	(U4)
*set *v.* 使做出坚定的表情	(U2)	*spirit *n.* 精神	(U2)
*settle *v.* 解决	(U6)	*spirit *n.* 灵魂，幽灵	(U3)
*share *n.* 份额	(U2)	*square *a.* 正直的	(U6)
shilling *n.* 先令	(U2)	stagger *v.* 踉跄	(U4)
shock *n.* 震惊	(U4)	*still *a.* 静止的	(U2)
shocked *a.* 震惊的	(U3)	sting *v.* 叮	(U3)
*sight *n.* 视域，眼界	(U6)	*strict *a.* 严格的	(U1)
*sink *v.* 堕落	(U8)	*strike *v.* 袭击	(U5)
*situation *n.* 情况	(U7)	*swear *v.* 发誓	(U2)
solve *v.* 解决	(U1)	*sword *n.* 剑	(U3)
son-in-law *n.* 女婿	(U7)		

T

tackle *v.* 解决	(U1)	think over 反复考虑	(U6)
the other day 几天以前	(U4)	Thornfield *n.* 桑菲尔德庄园	(U2)

throw in 外送，额外奉送	(U6)	*trade n. 交易，贸易	(U6)
*thunder n. 打雷，雷响	(U5)	*tutor v. 教导	(U7)

U

uncommon a. 不寻常的	(U6)	unnatural a. 反常的	(U3)
underworld n. 地狱	(U3)	unpleasant a. 不愉快的	(U6)
*unfair a. 不公平的	(U7)		

V

*valuable a. 有价值的	(U6)	villain n. 恶棍	(U3)
vanity n. 虚荣心	(U4)	vision n. 视力，看见的事物	(U3)
vibration n. 颤动	(U5)		

W

*wander v. 徘徊，流浪	(U8)	*wild a. 狂乱的	(U2)
*wealth n. 财富	(U2)	*will n. 意愿	(U2)
*wedding n. 婚礼	(U4)	*will n. 遗嘱	(U7)
wig n. 假发	(U4)	*willing a. 愿意的	(U7)

附录

如何排练英语短剧

英语短剧是中学生英语学习的一种有效手段。尽管中学生不可能像专业戏剧演员那样，接受严格的系统训练，但让他们学习一些演戏的常识，以提高演出水平，则是完全可以做到的。

1. 理解剧本

剧本是一出戏的基础文本，是剧作者的创作成果，被称为"一度创作"。剧本是演员塑造人物形象的依据。因此，在演出之前，要了解剧本的故事梗概，找出剧本的中心事件、主要矛盾和高潮，并分析剧本的主题思想，才能准确地把握角色在事件中的地位和态度，塑造人物的典型性格。学生在学习英语剧本时，应该查单词，做笔记。不管是自己的台词还是别人的台词，要将每一句话的意思都理解清楚，并弄清每句话的感情色彩。

2. 认识角色

当学生对剧本有了全面的了解之后，就要进而对自己所扮演的角色进行一番分析。

第一，了解角色的基本情况及其在剧本中的地位和作用。角色的基本情况有时出现在人物表里的介绍部分；有时在剧本里对人物有所提示；没有提示的，等看完剧本之后，也能归纳出角色的基本情况了。一出戏有不同的角色，其地位有轻重，作用有大小，凡是担任角色的，都要认真对待。

第二，分析角色的任务和贯穿行动线。明确角色任务的作用，是为了使舞台上的一言一语、一举一动都有明确的目的和方向。贯穿行动线是指演员在戏剧情节发展中的一系列的舞台行动。正因为每一个动作、表情和台词之间都有着必然的联系，这就自然形成了一条行动线。找到这条行动线，演员的表演才会有目的性，才能达到预期的效果。

第三，分析角色的性格特征。每个人都生活在一定的社会环境中，因此首先要分析角色具有的社会特征。其次要从角色的舞台行动来分析性格，即从剧本为角色提供的语言、行动和动作中去寻找角色的性格。另外还要从戏剧矛盾中分析人物性格。戏剧中人物的性格，随着剧情的逐渐发展而不断发展。在戏剧矛盾冲突最尖锐时，人物的性格也就展示得最充分。

为了充分理解角色，学生可以为角色写一个小传。角色小传就是把这个角色的家庭出身、经济状况、社会关系，以及这个角色的语言行动、兴趣爱好等等，按照剧本的提示，做一个比较全面和系统的设想，从这个设想中来分析人物的性格。

3. 说好台词

台词是戏剧表演的主要手段。怎么样才算好的台词呢？好的台词要语音纯正，口齿清楚，声音响亮，准确生动，达意传情，闻其声如见其人。那么怎样才能说好台词呢？

首先要熟悉台词。不光要熟悉自己这个角色的台词，还要熟悉整个剧情以及与自己角色有交流、有关系的角色的台词。要反复看、反复朗读、反复琢磨，要在完全理解的基础上来熟记。

其次要明确台词中标点符号的运用。标点符号能帮助演员分析语句的结构，辨明语气。语言的停顿、间隙、延长，延期的肯定、否定、反问、惊讶及感叹等，都可以从标点符号中反映出来。

最后，要对台词进行艺术处理，即根据人物的性格特点，找到这个人物特有的语气、语调和声音造型，并运用轻重缓急、高低快慢、抑扬顿挫等方法，对每一句台词进行节奏、重音、强调方面的处理。重音掌握不好，就会使语意不清；节奏不作处理，就会平铺直叙；没有强调，语气就会没有变化。演员用什么样的声音来说话好呢？一般来说，可以根据剧本的提示，根据角色的年龄、性格、气质和习惯等来加以区别。至于演员应用多大的音量来表演，可以遵循这样几条原则：第一，从生活出发。舞台上的说话，要尊重说话的自然规律，不要拿腔拿调或大喊大叫，又不能过于自然。舞台上的语言比生活中的语言夸张，音量比生活中要大一些，速度也要稍微慢一些。第二，从感情出发，从剧本规定情景出发。第三，从人物的性格来确定角色的音量。粗犷的性格可以用大嗓门儿，文静的性格则要用适中、柔和的声音。

4. 选择形体动作

选择舞台形体动作，是演员创造角色的另一个主要手段。戏剧动作有如下特点：第一，必须来源于生活，以生活中的真实动作为基础，既要自然逼真，又要有所夸张，动作可以稍微大一些，动作的节奏要与角色内心感情的节奏相适应。第二，从人物的性格出发。每一个人的外部动作都是性格和内心活动的表现。冷静果断的人处理复杂问题时在外部形体动作上会有很坚决、果断的手势或其他部位的动作，而优柔寡断的人在外部形体动作上，就会束手无策、摸头搓手。第三，从规定情景出发。即设计动作不能脱离剧本的规定情景，使动作既符合人物的行动目的，又符合事件发生的时间、地点、具体环境与条件等。第四，结合道具选择动作。在戏剧舞台上，道具可分为大道具、小道具。大道具指桌子、椅子、床、沙发等，小道具指手中的随身道具，如雨伞、毛巾、书等。演员可通过使用道具的不同动作来展现人物性格。

5. 进行排练

在排练前要找好代用道具。排练场的环境要按照剧本的规定情景来安排和布置。在做好上述准备工作后，就可以在导演（教师）的安排下，进入初排阶段。一般来说，初排就是"搭架子"，使每个演员对每场戏以及全剧事件有个形象的感受。演员要搞清楚上下场关系及来龙去脉，记住与自己有交流的角色，努力适应对方的表演，并把自己设计的动作、表情等在初排时实践一下。

接着进入细排阶段。细排就是在原来初排的基础上，更深入细致地理解剧本和角色。在细排时，要注意以下几个问题：第一是要注意外部动作的准确性，并把握好内部动作（即内心感情）的分寸。第二是要注意在舞台上与其他角色的交流。这包括感情、动作、台词上的交流。好的交流能使演员之间达成默契，推动剧情向前发展。第三就是合乐排练。要与音乐伴奏或其他音响效果准确地配合。如果配合不好，不光影响演员的表演，还会影响观众的情绪，甚至还会产生与剧情相反的反应。

下一步就是连排。连排就是经过了分段排练和细排之后进行的连贯性排练。连贯性主要体现在戏剧情节、人物行动线和感情的连贯上。演员在台上要明确角色的任务，在台下要弄清角色的去向，再一次上场要明白剧情前后的关系。

然后是彩排。彩排时，灯光、服装、道具、效果等都要尽可能地用上，这样角色的自我感觉就更强烈了。在彩排时，演员应做好一切准备，包括化装、服装、道具等；同时要具有自信心。有了自信心，演员就不会怯台，身体的各个部分都会比较松弛，动作起来也比较自然。有了自信心，才能深入角色，准确表达角色的感情。要克服怯台的现象，应注意平时多加练习，提高对剧本和角色的熟悉程度。另外要努力做到"心中有人，目中无人"。"心中有人"是说演员心中要有角色。演员上台之后，心中只有角色在行动，这样就可以使演员排除杂念、思想集中；"目中无人"是说演员在演戏时眼睛不能具体地看着某一个或某些观众。看得太具体，容易分神，容易跳出角色。

最后就是正式演出。在演出时如遇到意外的情况，如忘记台词、音响效果出差错等情况，不要随意中断演出，而是应该根据当时的情况进行灵活处理，尽量不要影响整个演出的进行。

英语教师在指导学生排练英语短剧时，在遵循上述排戏规律的基础上，应注意多发挥学生的主动性和创造性，让他们在这个过程中，最大限度地体会到英语学习的乐趣和戏剧表演的魅力。